鲁迅美术学院学术著作出版基金资助出版

实用英文翻译——理论、技巧与应用

齐 石◎著

新华出版社

图书在版编目 (CIP) 数据

实用英文翻译：理论、技巧与应用 / 齐石著 . --
北京：新华出版社，2022.12

ISBN 978-7-5166-6623-4

Ⅰ. ①实… Ⅱ. ①齐… Ⅲ. ①英语 – 翻译 – 研究
Ⅳ. ① H315.9

中国版本图书馆 CIP 数据核字（2022）第 233921 号

实用英文翻译：理论、技巧与应用

著　　者：齐　石

责任编辑：蒋小云　　　　　　　　　　　封面设计：马静静

出版发行：新华出版社

地　　址：北京石景山区京原路 8 号　　　邮　　编：100040

网　　址：http : //www.xinhuapub.com

经　　销：新华书店

　　　　　新华出版社天猫旗舰店、京东旗舰店及各大网店

购书热线：010-63077122　　　　　　　中国新闻书店购书热线：010-63072012

照　　排：北京亚吉飞数码科技有限公司

印　　刷：北京亚吉飞数码科技有限公司

成品尺寸：155mm × 235mm

印　　张：13.5　　　　　　　　　　　　字　　数：214 千字

版　　次：2023 年 6 月第一版　　　　　　印　　次：2023 年 6 月第一次印刷

书　　号：ISBN 978-7-5166-6623-4

定　　价：78.00 元

前　言

　　翻译是人类社会最悠久的活动之一,几乎与语言同时诞生。从原始部落的亲善交往到今天世界各国之间各个领域的频繁交流与往来,再到维护世界的持久稳定与和平,翻译都发挥了极其重要的作用。

　　美国语言学家、翻译家、翻译理论家尤金·奈达曾指出,翻译是指从语义到文体在译语中用最切近而最自然的对等话语再现原语的信息。我国著名翻译家傅雷先生认为,翻译应做到两点:首先理解要"化为我有",然后表达要"传神达意"。从这两位翻译家的表达中可见,翻译就是一门艺术,是语言的再创作艺术。

　　本书涵盖了理论、基础与技巧以及应用三个方面,虽侧重翻译,但同时也是一本不错的英语学习入门书,毕竟即便不从事专业的翻译工作,在英语学习中,理解和翻译能力也是最重要的能力之一。书中介绍了基础的翻译理论;实用的英文基础知识;易掌握的翻译技巧以及丰富的文字素材,可以帮助大家从基础入手,较科学、快速地改进翻译理念并提高翻译能力。

　　由于时间和笔者的水平有限,书中难免有不足和疏漏之处,敬请读者批评指正,提出宝贵意见。

作　者

2021 年 3 月

目 录

第一章　翻译概论　　　　　　　　　　　　1

第二章　如何成为词汇大师　　　　　　　　5

　第一节　古英语　　　　　　　　　　　　5

　第二节　英文词根　　　　　　　　　　　8

　第三节　构词成分　　　　　　　　　　　58

　第四节　英文词缀　　　　　　　　　　　63

　第五节　分类应用　　　　　　　　　　　65

第三章　翻译的语法观　　　　　　　　　　115

　第一节　主语的设置　　　　　　　　　　115

　第二节　主动与被动　　　　　　　　　　116

　第三节　及物与不及物　　　　　　　　　116

　第四节　冠　词　　　　　　　　　　　　117

　第五节　时态的另一面　　　　　　　　　118

　第六节　条件句　　　　　　　　　　　　118

　第七节　情态动词　　　　　　　　　　　119

　第八节　介　词　　　　　　　　　　　　120

　第九节　动副词组　　　　　　　　　　　120

第十节　直接、间接宾语　　　　　　　121
第十一节　尾部重量　　　　　　　　　123

第四章　翻译技巧　　　　　　　　　　**124**

第一节　长定语的翻译　　　　　　　　124
第二节　无主句的翻译　　　　　　　　125
第三节　替代词的使用　　　　　　　　126
第四节　尾　重　　　　　　　　　　　127
第五节　三段式翻译　　　　　　　　　128
第六节　插入语　　　　　　　　　　　129
第七节　句子成分转换　　　　　　　　130
第八节　填词、省略法　　　　　　　　131
第九节　分类使用词汇　　　　　　　　132
第十节　动名词的翻译　　　　　　　　133
第十一节　减译法　　　　　　　　　　133

第五章　习惯用语翻译　　　　　　　　**136**

第一节　押韵法　　　　　　　　　　　137
第二节　对比法　　　　　　　　　　　140
第三节　特殊结构法　　　　　　　　　141

第六章　文　化　　　　　　　　　　　**143**

第七章　教　育　　　　　　　　　　　**157**

第八章　经　济　　　　　　　　　　　**171**

第九章　科　技　　　　　　　　　　　**184**

第十章　艺　术　　　　　　　　　　　**195**

第一章　翻译概论

任何一种翻译活动,不论从内容方面(政治、社会、科技、艺术等)还是从形式方面(口译、笔译、同声传译)都具有鲜明的符号转换和文化传播的属性。作为文化和语言的转换活动,翻译的目的是沟通思想、交换信息,进而实现人类文明成果的共享。没有翻译作为媒介,文化、传统、科技的推广就无从谈起,所以翻译是人类社会共同进步的加速器。

从文化的角度来说,东西方对文化的理解有共同之处。在汉代的《说苑·指武》中第一次记载了该词,指出:"文化不改,武功加诛。"这里的"文化"与"武功"相对,有文治教化的意思。英语中文化(culture)一词来自拉丁语的 cultura,是耕种、养殖的意思,应该是自然科学的术语,而其代表人类社会文明的含义在19世纪初才进入英文。但现在文化这一社会属性已经成为人们对这个单词的主要认知。文化具有动态的特点,由于经济的发展、科技的进步,文化的内涵也随之发生改变。例如,互联网和电子媒体技术的发展,带来了网络文化的繁荣,才有了今天的各式各样网络语言和网络文化的产生。对于翻译活动的参与者而言,随时掌握文化的动态,既要了解世界文化,又要及时跟进掌握母语文化是从事这一行业的基本要求。所以,所有翻译从业人员应该对政治、科技、经济、社会和时事等保持足够的兴趣，随时了解最新信息，才能在翻译实践中做到游刃有余。

从语言的角度来说，我们首先要了解语言的本质。《韦氏新世界词典》（*Webster's New World Dictionary*）对语言的定义有如下几条：

人类语言（human speech）：人们通过这个手段进行交际（the ability to communicate by this means）；是一种语音和语义相结合的系统，用来表达和交流思想感情（a system of vocal sounds and combinations of such sounds to which meaning is attributed, used for the expression or communication of thoughts and feelings）；系统的书写形式（the written representation of such a system）；是表达或交流的手段：如手势、各种标识和动物发出的声音（any means of expressing or communicating, as gestures, signs, or animal sounds）。

语言的功能是通过语音、文字等符号赋予外部世界以意义。相同的事物或事件在不同文化中会引起不同的感受。语言的功能包括心理学和社会学的功能。语言的心理学功能表现在：是人们用来与客观世界沟通的手段，是人们认知外部世界的心理过程，可以细分为命名功能、陈述功能、表达功能、认知功能和建模功能五种。

命名功能即使用语言来对客观世界的事物给予定义和说明，当我们遇到一个新的事物时，出于本能的需要就是要知道具体怎样对其进行称谓。这一心理需求从幼儿时期就产生，并逐渐发展。

陈述功能指的是语言被用来说明事物和事物之间的关系，人们通过语言来说明一些事件和事物，以及它们之间的复杂关系。

表达功能是指人们自己的思想情感通过语言来进行对外传递。

语言的认知功能表现在它是人类思考的手段和媒介。人们的思维活动是以语言作为载体的，这就是为什么我们翻译时，看到一个单词，最初的反应是它在我们母语中的语义，而不是它所代表的具体事物的形象。

最后是语言的建模功能。建模功能指的是语言是被用来构建反映客观世界的认知图式的手段，比如原始人对树的认知只是孤单的一种存在,而随着人类认知能力的提升,我们会发现树有很多品种,而且脑子里也有了各种树的形象图形。

语言还具有社会学功能,它是人际沟通的手段,包括交流、信息获取、描述和煽情等。人们通过语言可以维系和改善与他人的关系;人们通过语言来获取知识,所以语言就有了信息获取的功能;语言还被用来发出指令、请求、提醒和告诫等,如各种军队的命令、母亲对孩子的告诫提醒等;语言还被用来说服社交对象,激发人的情感,影响人的情绪等,这是语言的煽情功能。在翻译当中,译者应该注意在传译这些功能的时候会出现的用词、语调等的变化,从而更加传神地将信息传递给目标人群。

翻译本身是个笼统的概念,可以划分为口译(interpretation)、笔译(translation)、机器翻译(machine translation)和机助翻译(machine-aided translation)。在口译中又有交替传译(consecutive interpretation)和同声传译(simultaneous interpretation)。将外国语言翻译为母语称为"里译",将母语翻译成目标外语称为"外译"。

翻译的标准有很多,但基本的共识是要达到"信、达、雅"这三个标准。"信"即对原文的忠实,翻译是不可以随意发挥和篡改原作者的语义和情感的。"达"是指翻译的内容要使读者或听者充分准确地理解,令人迷惑不解的译文是不合格的。"雅"是指语言的优美,能让人产生美感。当然,"雅"应该是建立在"信"和"达"的基础之上的,没有对原文含义的"信"和表达的通顺,"雅"就没有任何意义了。

翻译中的口译具有即时性的特点,译者往往没有充足的时间做准备,要根据现场情况及时、准确地理解和传达,因此译者需具有更加强大的心理素质和更加广博的知识存储。另外,也有一些对译员的心理和生理条件的要求,比如比较胆怯的性格特点,或者有先天性语病的(口吃、发音障碍等)就不适合担当口译工作。笔译的从业者则要从不同的方面来考虑。

首先笔译要求翻译内容更加准确和优美,为此,译员应该做好充分的准备,包括对原文作者的了解、对材料背景和相关专业知识的学习和准备。只有做足了功课,才能确保对原文语义的精确理解。表达是笔译的第二步,表达的准确程度依赖于对原文的理解程度。最后还要对翻译的内容进行校对,确保没有笔误,不遗失信息。

翻译的方法可以简单分成意译和直译。意译指的是译者只忠实于原文的语义,而不拘泥于原文的表现形式。因为中外文化的巨大差异,很多词语和表达法在另一种语言中完全不存在,或部分存在,这样就要求译者对原文语义有更加全局性的把握,从而在不改变基本语义的情况下,对表达方式做出适当的调整。而直译法则既能保持原文的语义又能保持原文的形式,包括原文的修辞手段和基本结构,从而既表达了语义,又保留一定的原汁原味儿的异国情调。在具体翻译实践中,不能僵硬地保持意译或直译的风格,采用哪种方式一定是视情况而定的,取决于原文的特点。在绝大多数情况下,需要两种翻译方式的结合,才能创作出理想的译文。

最后想谈一下译者基本素质的修炼。首先当然是译者要有较高的外语水平,只有这样才能从理解和表达的角度做到准确无误。其次译者还要有扎实的汉语基础,这和要有雄厚的外语基础是同样的道理。除此以外,译者还应该具有广博的知识储备、丰富的翻译经验和认真的工作态度。只有具备了上述条件,才能成为一名优秀的翻译工作者。

第二章　如何成为词汇大师

词汇能力是一名译者最基础的能力,尤其在口译过程中,译员没有时间去查阅工具书,因此,其储存的词汇量就变成了决胜关键。可以毫不夸张地说"得词汇者得天下"。强大的词汇能力表现在两个方面:一是要熟知如何掌握词汇,二是知道如何使用词汇。我们大多数英语学习者都有"重"词汇量,"轻"词汇"质"的特点,也就是说相对地不太注意如何使用英文词汇。本章从词汇的掌握和词汇的使用两个方面来介绍翻译中的词汇问题。

第一节　古英语

我们知道英语的词汇有着不同的历史发展阶段。首先是古英语阶段,即来自日耳曼的盎格鲁和撒克逊部落来到英伦三岛,与当地的凯尔特语融合而成了古英语。古英语单词在现代英语中还留存大约不到三千单词,但这两千多词汇已成为英语的骨干词汇,任意一篇英文文章或讲稿中 70% 左右的词汇都来自古英语单词。英国的语言学家专门为旅行者和在英语国家短期工作者提供了一份 "850 basic" 的英语基础词汇表,基本可以在英语国家进行简单的交流；美国的七家字典编撰单位通过计算机运算得出了 1200 个最常用的英文名词和动词，以及 300 个最常用的形容词，并明确说明，这 1500 个单词就是在英语国家日常生活所需的基本词汇。

这些基础词汇的特点是：（1）生活常用词汇。任何一种语言，在诞生初期一定是以生活中不可或缺的人或物的称谓作为基础词汇的。首先满足物质生活，再去考虑精神世界，所以人称、天气、日期时间、衣食住行等一定是最先出现的词汇。（2）字母较少。在语言出现的早期，一定不会有复杂的构词方式，更多是以方便、容易掌握和记忆为优先考虑而创造出的词汇，所以 3 ~ 5 个字母构成的单词就成了英语基础词汇（古英语词汇）的特征。（3）在交流中使用英语的基础词汇可以拉近情感距离。不要想当然地认为使用这些基础词汇就暴露出语言能力不足。我们需要了解的是：英语是一个注重沟通实效、强调言简意赅的语言。它不过多地追求语言的华丽，而以简单明了作为优先考虑，所以简单的单词反倒能引起情感共鸣。英国首相丘吉尔，同时也是诺贝尔文学奖获得者曾说过"若一篇演讲中大多采用单音节的古英语词汇，就很容易唤起听者的强烈共鸣"。第二次世界大战期间，他的那篇动员英国人民奋力抵抗纳粹入侵的著名演讲中使用的基本都是古英语词汇，语言铿锵有力、掷地有声，激起英国人强烈的民族自豪感，极大地鼓舞了士气、振奋了人心。（4）多功能性。古英语的词汇往往能一词多用，这部分单词很多都可以既作名词，又作动词，还可以作形容词、副词，甚至介词。实际上，一名出色的翻译应玩转这部分单词，别忘了这两千多个单词可是占据了任意一篇文章的 70% 左右的内容。

以下，按字母顺序选取了一些单词以展示古英语单词的特点：

ache after again ail air amaze any ape apple ask
baby back bad bag bake bait bald ball band bare
call can care cat chalk cheap cheat cheek chest chew
dairy daisy dare dark darling day dead deaf deal dear
each ear early earn earth east eat ebb edge eel
fair fall false fan far fare fart fast fat father

gall game gang garlic gate gather get ghost giddy gird

hack hail hair half hall ham hammer hand handle hang

ice idle if in inch inner it itch inchmeal indeed（字母"I"下全部古英语单词）

字母"J"下没有古英语单词。

keen keep ken kettle key kind king kiss kitchen kite

lady lake lame ladder lamb land lane lap lark last

mad maiden main make malt man mane manifold mantle many maple

nail naked name nap narrow navel neat neck need needle

oak oar oat oath of off offer oft old on

palm pan parsley part past path peacock pear penny peony

queen quench quick quake quaver quell quiver（字母 Q 下全部古英语单词）

race rain rake rainbow ram rat rather raw reach read

sack sad saddle sail sake sale sallow salt salve sand

table tail take tale tall tame tan tap tape tar

under understand undo up upright（字母"U"下全部古英语单词）

字母 V 下没有古英语单词。

wade wake walk wall wallow wander wane war ward ware

字母 X 下没有古英语单词。

yard yarn yawn year yell yellow yelp yes yet yield yoke you young

字母 Z 下没有古英语单词。

笔者将一些常用古英语单词编成顺口溜儿，请大家感受下这些"小单词"的"大功效"。

Take make have get go

Break work give let grow

Come say put stay hold

Win lose gain keep flow

Good and bad high and low

Thin and fat fast and slow
Easy and hard new and old
Alive and dead warm and cold

Life and death heart and soul
Danger and safety waste and gold
Head and foot hand and elbow
Sky and ground friend and foe

Bring words together you will see no end
Tired people be till the neck bend
Learning something god will not lend
Remain study worth the time spent（共 78 词）

第二节　英文词根

随着基督教的传入，古希腊文明的"入侵"，外来语大量进入了英文，英语的词汇量也随之爆炸式增长。拉丁语和希腊语有一个共同的特点，即词根构词法。由一个词根（word root）加上构词成分（combining form）构成。此类词汇与我国汉字的偏旁部首构成方式有异曲同工之妙。因此针对这部分单词，我们的掌握方式应该是分析式（analytical）。当我们积累了一定量的词根、构词成分信息，就会发现记忆并掌握单词是有一定技巧的。经过分析，将较实用的词根整理如下：

1.acro

表达语义：topmost; high

例词：

acrobat：杂技 acro + bat = topmost + walk

acronym：缩写 acro + nym = topmost + name

acropolis：卫城 acro + polis = high + city

2.ambi

表达语义：around

例词：

ambient：周围的 ambi + ent = around + ent（此处为形容词后缀）

ambiguous：模糊不清的 ambi + gu + ous = around + drive + ous（形容词后缀）

ambition：雄心 ambi + it + tion = around + go + tion（名词后缀）

ambivalent：矛盾情绪 ambi + val + ent = both + strong + ent（此处为形容词后缀）

3.amphi

表达语义：around；on both sides

例词：

amphibian：两栖的 amphi + bi + an = on both sides + life + an（此处为形容词后缀）

4.an

表达语义：not；without

例词：

anarchy：无政府 an + arch + y = without + rule + y（名词后缀）

anecdote：轶事 an + ec（ex）+ dote = not + out + given

ambrosia：美味食物 am + brosia = not + mortal

5.ante

表达语义：before，opposite to，post

例词：

antecedent：先行的 ante + ced + ent = before + go + ent（此处为形容词词缀）

antemeridian：上午的 ante + meri + dian = before + middle + day

antenuptial：婚前的 ante + nuptial = before + wedding

6.arch

表达语义：chief；old

例词：

architect：建筑师 archi + tect = chief + builder

archaeology：考古学 archae + ology = old + study

7.auto

表达语义：self

例词：

autocracy：独裁制度 auto + cracy = self + rule

autogamy：动植物自生 auto + gamy = self + marriage

autogenous：自生的 auto + gen + ous = self + born + ous（形容词后缀）

automate：使自动 auto + mate = self + think

autopsy：验尸 auto + psy = self + sight

autotomy：（动物遭受攻击时）自行切除身体 auto + tom + y = self + cut + y（名词后缀）

8.bene

表达语义：well;（good opposite to mal）

例词：

benediction：祝福 bene + dic + tion = well + say + tion（名词后缀）

benefaction：善行 bene + fac + tion = well + do + tion（名词后缀）

beneficial：有利的 bene + fic + ial = well + do + ial（此处为形容词后缀）

benevolent：善意的；慈善的 bene + vol + ent = good + wish + ent（此处为形容词后缀）

benign：善良的 beni + gn = well + gn

9.bi

表达语义：double; two

例词：

bigamy：重婚 bi + gamy = double + marriage

binocular：双目的 bi + ocul + ar = two + eye + ar（此处为形容词缀）

bipartisan：两党的 bi + parti + san = two + party + man（此处为形容词后缀）

10.bibl

表达语义：book

例词：

Bible：圣经

bibliography：参考书目 bibl + iograpy = book + writing

bibliomania：藏书癖 bibl + io + mania = book + crazy

11.cata

表达语义：down；downward；fully

例词：

cataclysm：大洪水；大地震 cata + clysm = down + wash

catadromous：为产卵而顺流入海 cata + drom + ous = down + run + ous（形容词后缀）

catalogue：目录 cata + logue = fully + say，tell

catalyst：催化剂 cata + lyst = down + free

cataract：瀑布 cata + ract = down + break（瀑布，洪流）

catastasis：叙述；高潮 cata + sta + sis = down +stand + sis（名词后缀）

catastrophe：灾难 cata + strophe = down + turning

catatonia：紧张症 cata + tonia = down + tension

category：种类 cat + egory = down + assembly

12.circum

表达语义：around

例词：

circumcise：割礼 circum + cise = around + cut

circumference：圆周 circum + fer + ence = around + carry + ence（名词后缀）

circumfuse：浇灌；围绕 circum + fuse = around + pour（散布，灌溉）

circumjacent：周边的 circum + jac + ent = around + throw + ent（此处为形容词后缀）

circumlocution：迂回的说法 circum + locu + tion = around + speak + tion（名词后缀）

circumnavigate：环绕航行 circum + navigate = around + sail

circumspect：细心；慎重的 circum + spect = around + look

circumstance：情况 circum + stan + ce = around + stand + ce（名词后缀）

circuit：circu + it = around + go

13.com

表达语义：together; with; wholly（变型：co, con, col, comb, cor, coun）

例词：

combat：战斗 com + bat = with + fight

combine：结合；融合 com + bine = together + bind

comfort：安慰 com + fort = together + strong

commence：开始 com + mence = together + initiate

commiserate：同情 com + miser + ate = together + sad + ate（此处为动词后缀）

common：普遍；共同的 com + mon = together + duties

commotion：暴动 com + mot + ion = together + move + ion（名词后缀）

compatriot：同胞 com + patri + ot = together + father + ot（名词缀）

compile：编辑 com + pile = together + heap

compose：创作 com + pose = together + put

coadunate：联合的 co + ad + unate = together + to + unite

coalesce：合并 co + al + esce = together + grow + esce（名词后缀）

coalition：联盟 co + ali + tion = together + grow + tion（名词后缀）

coerce：强制 co + erce = together + restrain

coeval：同时代的 co + ev + al = together + age + al（此处为形容词后缀）

cohere：附着；一致 co + here = together + stick

coincide：一致；巧合 co + incide = together + fall upon

collaborate：合作 col + labor + ate = together + work + ate（此处为形容词后缀）

collapse：崩溃 col + lapse = together + fall down

collide：冲撞 col + lide = together + strike

collimate：校准 col + lim + ate = together + make straight + ate（此处为动词后缀）

collinear：共线的 col + line + ar = together + line + ar（形容词后缀）

collusion：共谋；勾结 col +lus + ion = together + play + ion（名词后缀）

concave：凹陷 con + cave = together + hollow

conceit：自负 con + ceit = together + take

concentrate：集中 con + centr + ate = together + center + ate（此处为动词后缀）

conclude：结论 con + clude = together + shut

concoct：同谋 con + coct = together + cook

concord：协和 con + cord = together + heart

concourse：集合；总汇 con+ course = together + run

condemn：谴责 con+ demn = together + harm

condole：哀悼 con + dole = together + grief

confederate：同盟；联合 con + feder + ate = together + league + ate（此处为动词后缀）

confer：授予 con+ fer = together + carry

configuration：结构；配置 con + figure + ate = wholly + form + ation（名词后缀）

confiscate：没收 con + fisc + ate = wholly + treasury + ate（此处为动词后缀）

confront：面对 con + front = with + forehead

confute：驳斥 con + fute = together + beat

congenial：协调一致的 con + geni + al = together + inborn nature + ial（此处为形容词后缀）

consume：消费 con + sume = wholly + take

contaminate：污染；弄脏 con + tamin + ate = together + touch + ate（此处为动词后缀）

correct：纠正 cor + rect = wholly + right

corrupt：腐败 cor + rupt = together + break

14.de

表达语义：down；downward

例词：

debate：辩论 de + bate = down + beat

debris：碎片；残骸 de + bris = down + break

decadence：颓废 de + cadence = down + falling

decapitate：斩首 de + capit + ate = down，off + head + ate（此处为动词后缀）

decease：去世 de + cease = off + go

deceive：欺骗 de + ceive = from + take

decide：决定 de + cide = off + cut

defect：缺点 de + fect = down + do

depict：描述 de + pict = fully + paint

derive：源于 de + rive = away + stream

devastate：破坏 de + vast + ate = fully + waste + ate（此处为动词后缀）

devour：吞没 de + vour = fully + eat

15.deca

表达语义：ten

例词：

decagon：十角形 deca + gon = ten + angle

16.demi

表达语义：half

例词：

demigod：半人半神 demi + god = half + god

17.dia

表达语义：across；between；through

例词：

diacritical：区分的 dia + crit + ical = between + separate + ical（形容词后缀）

diagnosis：诊断 dia + gno + sis = between + know + sis（名词后缀）

diagonal：对角的 dia + gon + al = through + cross + angle + al（此处为形容词后缀）

diagram：图解；图表 dia + gram = through + writing

dialect：方言 dia + lect = between + choose

dialogue：对话 dia + logue = between + speech

18.dis

表达语义：apart；away；not

例词：

dispose：处理 dis + pose = apart + place

disrupt：分裂 dis + rupt = apart + break

dissect：切开 dis + sect = away + cut

dissent：异议 dis + sent = away + think

digest：消化 di + gest = apart + carry

diffident：无自信的 di + ffid + ent：= apart + trust + ent（此处为形容词后缀）

diverge：分歧；岔开 di + verge = apart + bend

19.duo

表达语义：double；two（变型：do，dou，du）

例词：

dozen：12 一打 do + zen = two + ten

20.epi

表达语义：among；besides；to；upon

例词：

epidemic：流行病 epi + dem + ic = among + people + ic（形容词后缀）

epigraph：碑文；题词 epi + graph = upon + write

21.eu

表达语义：well（变型：ev）

例词：

eugenics：优生学 eu +geni + cs = well + born + cs（名词后缀）

eulogy：颂词 eu + logy = well + speak

euthanasia：安乐死 eu + thanas + is = well + die + ia（名词后缀）

22.ex

表达语义：fully；out of（变化型：e；es）

例词：

exceed：超出 ex + ceed = out + go

excel：出色 ex + cel = out + rise

except：除外 ex + cept = out + take

excerpt：摘录 ex + crept = out + pick

exempt：免除 ex + empt = out + take

exert：发挥；施加影响 ex + ert = out + put together

exhaust：排放 ex + haust = out + draw

exhilarate：兴高采烈 ex + hilar + ate = out + glad + ate（此处为动词后缀）

exhort：劝诫 ex + hort = out + urge

exhume：发掘 ex + hume = out + ground

exit：出口 ex + it = out + go

expire：期满；呼出 ex + pire = out + breathe

expound：详细说明 ex + pound = out + put

explicit：外在的；直言的 ex + plicit = out + fold

exquisite：精致的 ex + quisite = out + sought

edit：编辑 e + dit = out + give

elaborate：详细说出 e + labor + ate = fully + work + ate（此处为动词后缀）

elect：选举 e + lect = out + choose

elide：省略 e + lide = out + strike

elicit：引出 e + licit = out + entice

elope：私奔 e + lope = out + run

erudite：博学的 e + rud + ite = fully + rude（nature）+ ite（此处为形容词后缀）

event：事件 e + vent = out + come

evident：明显 e + vid + dent = out + see + ent（此处为形容词后缀）

evoke：唤起 e + voke = out + call

23.hector

表达语义：hundred

例词：

hectogram：百克 hecto + gram = hundred + gram

24.hemi

表达语义：half

例词：

hemisphere：半球 hemi + sphere = half + ball

25.hetero

表达语义：other；different

例词：

Heterodox：异端的 hetero + dox = different + opinion

26.in

表达语义：in；into；on（变型：il；ir，im）

例词：

incarnate：体现 in + carn + ate = in + flesh + ate（此处为动词后缀）

inceptive：起始的 in + cept + ive = in + take + ive（形容词后缀）

incident：事件 in + cid + ent = in + fall + ent（此处为名词后缀）

increase：增加 in + crease = in + grow

incriminate：连累 in + crimin + ate = into + crime + ate（此处为动词后缀）

infect：传染 in + fect = in + put

influence：影响 in + flu + ence = in + flow + ence（名词后缀）

ingrain：使根深蒂固 in + grain = in + nature

innovate：创新 in + nov + ate = in + new + ate（此处为动词后缀）

inquire：咨询 in + quire = into + seek

insert：插入 in + sert = in + join

instead：替代 in + stead = in + place

intuition：直觉 in + tui + tion = in + watch + tion（名词后缀）

illuminate：照亮 il + lumen + ate = on + light + ate（此处为动词缀）

involve：涉及；卷入 in + volve = in + roll

27.meta

表达语义：after；among；with（变化之意）

例词：

Metabolism：新陈代谢 meta + bol + ism = after + throw + ism（名词后缀）

28.ob

表达语义：at；against；before；near；over；towards（变型：o；oc；of；op；os）

例词：

obdurate：顽固的 ob + dur + ate = against + hard + ate（此处为形容词后缀）

obese：肥胖 ob + ese = over + eat

obscene：淫秽；猥琐 ob + scene = towards + filthy

obscure：模糊；昏暗 ob + scure = over + cover

obstacle：障碍 ob + sta + cle = against + stand + cle（名词后缀）

obtain：获得 ob + tain = near + hold

occur：出现 oc + cur = towards + run

offend：侵犯 of + fend = against + strike

offer：提供 of + fer = near + carry

29.omni

表达语义：all

例词：

omniscient：无所不知的 omni + scient = all + knowing

30.para

表达语义：against；beside；beyond；contrary（变型：par；pa）

例词：

paradox：悖论 para + dox = contrary + opinion

paragon：杰出典范 para + gon = beyond + sharp

paranoid：妄想症；偏执狂 para + noid = beside + mind

parasite：寄生虫 para + site = beside + food

parody：打油诗 par + ody = beside + ode

31.pen

表达语义：almost

例词：

peninsula：半岛 pen + isula = almost + island

32.per

表达语义：away；thoroughly；through（变化型：par；pel；pil）

例词：

perambulate：巡行 徘徊 per + ambul + ate = through + walk + ate（此处为动词后缀）

perceive：理解 per + ceive = thoroughly + take

percussion：打击乐 per + cuss + ion = thoroughly + strike + ion

perfect：完美 per + fect = thoroughly + make

perfidy：不诚实 per + fid + y = away + faith + y（此处为名词缀）

permanent：永远 per + man + ent = through + remain + ent（此处为形容词后缀）

permit：允许 per + mit = through + sent

perish：消亡 per + ish = thoroughly + go

perpetual：永恒的 per + pet + ual = through + seek + ual（形容词后缀）

persecute：迫害 per + secute = through + follow

perspective：角度；透视 per + spect + ive = through + see + ive（形容词后缀）

perspire：出汗 per + spire = through + breathe

persuade：说服 per + suade = thoroughly + advise

pertinent：中肯的；切题的 per + tin + ent = thoroughly + hold + ent（此处为形容词后缀）

pervade：弥漫 per + vade = through + go

pervert：堕落；反常 per + vert = thoroughly + turn

pilgrim：旅行；朝圣者 pil + grim = through + land

33.peri

表达语义：around

例词：

perimeter：周长 peri + meter = around + measure

period：时期；时段 peri + od = around + way

34.pro

表达语义：before; for; forth（变化型：pur; pr）

例词：

promise：承诺 pro + mise = forth + forward

profess：表白；声称 pro + fess = forth + acknowledge

propel：推进 pro + pel = forward + drive

protect：保护 pro + tect = before + cover

purpose：目的 pur + pose = before + put

35.prot（o）

表达语义：first

例词：

prototype：原型 proto + type = first + type

36.se

表达语义：apart; away

例词：

secede：脱离 se + cede = apart + go

seclude：隐退 se + clude = apart + shut

seduce：勾引 se + duce = apart + lead

segregate：隔离 se + greg + ate = apart + flock + ate

select：选择 se + lect = apart + choose

separate：分开 se + par + ate = apart + prepare + ate（此处
为动词后缀）

37.super

表达语义：above; over（变化型：sop; sove; sur）

例词：

surfeit：过度；沉溺于 sur + feit = over + do

surmise：推测 sur + mise = over + send

38.acu

表达语义：sour；sharp（变化型：acid；acr）

例词：

acuity：尖锐 acu + ity = sharp = ity（名词后缀）

acumen：敏锐 acu + men = sharp + men（名词后缀，与 ment 同源）

39.al

表达语义：nourish（变化型：ul；ol）

例词：

aliment：营养物 ali + ment = nourish + ment（名词后缀）

prolific：多产的 pr + oli + fic = forward + nourish + do

adolescence：青春期 ad + ole + scence = to + nourish + scence（名词后缀）

40.alg

表达语义：pain

例词：

analgesic：止痛的 an + alg +esic = no + pain + ic（形容词后缀）

neuralgia：神经痛 neur + alg + ia = nerve + pain + ia（名词后缀）

nostalgia：怀旧 nost + alg + ia = home + pain + ia（名词后缀）

41.alt

表达语义：high

例词：

altimeter：高度计 alt + meter = high + measure

altitude：高度 alt + itude + high + itude（名词后缀）

exalt：提升；赞扬 ex + alt = out + high

42.alter

表达语义：other（变化型：altr；altrus；ali，ulter）

例词：

altruism：利他主义 altru + ism = other + ism（名词后缀）

alienation：疏远；离间 ali + en + ation = other + en + ation（名词后缀）

alibi：不在场证明 ali + by = other + place

adultery：通奸 al + ulter + y = ad（强化语气）+ other + y（此处为名词后缀）

adulterate：掺杂 ad + ulter + ate = ad（强化语气）+ other + ate（此处为动词后缀）

43.am

表达语义：love（变化型：em；ama）

例词：

amatory：恋爱的；情人的 ama + tory = love + ory（名词后缀）

amicable：亲切 am + ic + able = love + ic + able（形容词后缀）

amiable：亲密 ami + able = love + able（形容词后缀）

amorist：谈情说爱的人 amor + ist = love + ist（名词后缀）

enamor：迷住 en + amor = into + love

44.anim

表达语义：soul

例词：

animate：动漫 anim + ate = soul + ate（此处为动词后缀）

magnanimous：宽宏大量的 magn + anim + ous = great + soul + ous（形容词后缀）

45.apt

表达语义：fit

例词：

aptitude：能力 apt + itude = fit + itude（名词后缀）

adaptive：适应的 ad + apt + ive = to + fit + ive（形容词后缀）

46.aqua

表达语义：water（变化型：aque；aqui）

例词：

aquacade：水上表演 aqua + cade = water + sight

aqueduct：水管；沟渠 aque + duct = water + lead

aquifer：含水层 aqui + fer = water + bearing

47.aud

表达语义：hear（变化型：audit）

例词：

auditorium：学术报告厅 audit + orium = hear + place

48.aug

表达语义：increase；to make grow（变化型：auc，au）

例词：

augment：增加 aug + ment = increase + ment（名词后缀，augment 此处为动词）

49.avi

表达语义：bird

例词：

aviculture：鸟类学 avi + culture = bird + nourish

50.bat

表达语义：go

例词：

acrobat：杂技 acro + bat = high + go

51.bell

表达语义：war

例词：

bellicose：好战的 belli + cose = war + cose（表"多"的形容词后缀）

belligerent：好战；交战的 belli + ger + ent = war + carry + ent（此处为形容词后缀）

rebel：反叛 re + bel = back + war

52.bio

表达语义：life

例词：

biopsy：活组织检查 bio +（o）psy = life + sight

biosphere：生物圈 bio + sphere = life + scope

symbiosis：共栖 sym + bio + sis = same + life + sis（名词后缀）

53.brev

表达语义：short（变化型：bridge）

例词：

abbreviate：缩写 ab + brev + iate = to + short + ate（此处为动词后缀）

54.cad

表达语义：fall（变化型：cid，cas）

例词：

decadence：颓废 de + cad + ence = down + fall + ence（名词后缀）

accident：事故 ac + cid + ent = to + fall + ent（此处为名词后缀）

cascade：瀑布 cas + cade = fall + sight

casualty：受伤 cas + ual + ty = fall + ual + ty（名词后缀）

55.calc

表达语义：lime（变化型：calx）

例词：

calcium：钙 culc + ium = lime + ium（表化学元素的名词后缀）

calculate：计算 calc + u + late = lime + ul + ate（此处为动词后缀）

56.cant

表达语义：sing（变化型：chant；cent）

例词：

descant：曲调；歌曲 des + cant = down + sing

accent：口音 ac + cent = to + sing

57.cap

表达语义：head；take

例词：

capable：能够 cap + able = take + able（形容词后缀）

58.carn

表达语义：flesh

例词：

carnage：大屠杀 carn + age = flesh + age（集合名词后缀）

carnal：肉体的；肉欲的 carn + al = flesh + al（形容词后缀）

carnivore：肉食动物 carni + vore = flesh + eat

59.cede

表达语义：go；yield（变化型：ceed；cess）

例词：

accede：同意 ac + cede = to + yield

antecedent：先行的 ante + ced + ent = before + go + ent（此处为形容词后缀）

concede：承认；让步 con + cede = with + yield

incessant：不间断；连续的 in + cess + ant = not + go away + ant（此处为形容词后缀）

intercede：说情；调节 inter + cede = between + go

recession：衰退 re + cess + ion = back + go + ion（名词后缀）

secede：脱离；分离 se + cede = away + go

60.ceive

表达语义：take（变化型：cept；cip cipate）

例词：

intercept：拦截 inter + cept = between + take

precept：规诫；格言 pre + cept = before + take

61.celer

表达语义：swift

例词：

accelerate：加速 ac + celer + ate = to swift + ate（此处为动词后缀）

decelerate：减速 de + celer + ate = down + swift + ate（此处为动词后缀）

62.cern

表达语义：separate（变化型：cret）

例词：

discern：辨别 dis + cern = apart + separate

discrete：不连续的；离散 dis + crete = apart + separate

63.cert

表达语义：sure

例词：

certitude：确定；确信 cert + itude = sure + itude（名词后缀）

disconcert：不和谐 dis + con + cert = apart + with + sure

64.chrom

表达语义：color

例词：

chromatin：色素 chromate + in = color + in（名词后缀）

65.chron

表达语义：time

例词：

Synchronous：同步 syn + chron + ous = same + time + ous（形容词后缀）

66.cide

表达语义：cut; kill（变化型：cise）

例词：

incise：切割 in + cise = in + cut

germicide：杀菌剂 germi + cide = germ + kill

67.cite

表达语义：call; urge

例词：

recite：背诵 re + cite = back + call

68.coct

表达语义：cook

例词：

concoct：捏造；编造 con + coct = together + cook

69.cognis

表达语义：know（变化型：gnos）

例词：

prognosis：预测；预后 pro + gno + sis = forward + know + sis（名词后缀）

70.cord

表达语义：heart（变化型：core）

例词：

concord：协和 con + cord = together + heart

cordiality：热忱 cord + ial + ty + heart + ial + ty（名词后缀）

discord：不和 dis + cord = apart + heart

71.corp

表达语义：body

例词：

corporeal：肉体的 corpor + eal = body + eal（形容词后缀）

72.cosm

表达语义：universe；order

例词：

cosmopolitan：世界性的；宽广的 cosmo + polit + an = universe + city + an（此处为形容词后缀）

73.cre

表达语义：make；grow（变化：cres）

例词：

accretion：自然增大；添加物 ac + cre + tion = to + grow + tion（名词后缀）

74.cred

表达语义：believe

例词：

credulous：轻信；易受骗的 cred + ul + ous = believe + much + ous（形容词后缀）

75.crit

表达语义：judge

例词：

Criterion：标准 crit + er + ion = judge + er + ion（名词后缀）

76.cult

表达语义：till

例词：

acculturate：适应新文化 ac + cultur + ate = to + till + ate（此处为动词后缀）

77.cumb

表达语义：lie；down

例词：

succumb：屈服 suc + cumb = downward + lie down

78.cur

表达语义：run

例词：

incur：招致 in + cur = in + run

79.cure

表达语义：take care

例词：

accuracy：准确 ac + cur + acy = to + take care + acy（名词后缀）

80.cuss

表达语义：strike; shake

例词：

repercussion：间接影响 re + per + cuss + ion = repeat + thorough + strike + ion（名词后缀）

81.dei

表达语义：god

例词：

deiform：似神的；有神性的 dei + form = god + form

82.dem

表达语义：people

例词：

endemic：地方病的 en + dem + ic = among + people + ic（形容词后缀）

demography：人口志 dem + graphy = people + write

pandemic：大规模传染病 pan + dem + ic = broad + people + ic（形容词后缀）

83.derm

表达语义：skin（变化型：derma; dermat）

例词：

dermatology：皮肤病学 derma + tology = skin + study

epidermis：表皮 epi + derm + is = upon + skin + is（名词后缀）

84.dict

表达语义：say（变化型：dit）

例词：

predict：预测 pre + dict = before + say

85.doc

表达语义：teach

例词：

doctrine：教义 doct + rine = teach + r + ine（名词后缀）

86.dom

表达语义：house；tame；rule

例词：

domestic：国内的；家内的 dom + es + tic = home + es + tic（形容词后缀）

87.don

表达语义：give（变化型：dot；dow）

例词：

endow：赋予 en + dow = in + give

donate：捐献 don + ate = give + ate（此处为动词后缀）

88.dorm

表达语义：sleep

例词：

dormant：睡眠状态的 dorm + ant = sleep + ant（此处为形容词后缀）

dormitory：宿舍 dorm + itory = sleep + itory（名词后缀）

89.dox

表达语义：opinion（变化型：dogma）

例词：

orthodox：正统 ortho + dox = straight + opinion

90.duce/duct

表达语义：lead；take

例词：

deduce：减去 扣除 de + duce = down + lead

91.dur

表达语义：hard；last

例词：

indurate：使硬化 in + dur + ate = into + hard + ate（此处为动词后缀）

92.dyn

表达语义：power（变化型：dynamo）

例词：

dynast：君主 dyn + ast = power + people

dynamo：发电机 dyn + amo = power + o（名词后缀）

93.eco

表达语义：house

例词：

ecotourism：生态旅游 eco + tourism = house + tourism

94.em

表达语义：take；buy（变化型：empt）

例词：

preempt：先买；先取 pre + empt = before + take

redeem：赎回；挽回 red + eem = back + take

95.equ/equi

表达语义：equal

例词：

equality：平等 equ + ality = equal + ality（名词后缀）

96.erg

表达语义：work（变化型：urg）

例词：

energy：能量 en + erg + y = into + work + y（名词后缀）

97.err

表达语义：wander；err

例词：

errant：离开正道；不定的 err + ant = wander + ant（形容词后缀）

aberrant：违反常规的 ab + err + ant = away + wander + ant（形容词后缀）

98.ess

表达语义：be（变化型：est）

例词：

essence：精华 ess + ence = be + ence（名词后缀）

99.fa

表达语义：speak（变化型：fam；fan；fat；fess）

例词：

fable：寓言 fa + ble = speak + ble

100.fac

表达语义：face；forehead（变化型：front）

例词：

efface：抹去；消除 ef + face = out + face

101.fact

表达语义：make；do（变化型：fect；fac）

例词：

factitious：人为的 fact + titious = make + titious（形容词后缀）

manufacture：制造 manu +facture = hand + make + ure（名词后缀）

facile：容易的 fac + ile = make + ile（形容词后缀）

102.fall

表达语义：deceive（变化型：fals）

例词：

fallacy：谬论 fall + acy = deceive + acy（名词后缀）

fallible：易错的 fall + ible = deceive + ible（形容词后缀）

103.fam

表达语义：speak

例词：

defamation：诽谤 de + fam + ation = down + speak + ation（名词后缀）

104.fare

表达语义：go

例词：

farewell：再见 fare + well = go + well

105.fend

表达语义：strike（变化型：fest）

例词：

infest：骚扰；寄生 in + fest = in + strike

106.fer

表达语义：carry；bear

例词：

ferriage：摆渡 fer + iage = carry + iage（名词后缀）

fertile：肥沃 fer + tile = carry + ile（形容词后缀）

confer：授予；赠予 con + fer = with + carry

defer：延期 de + fer = away + carry

infer：推论 in + fer = in + carry

107.fess

表达语义：speak

例词：

confess：坦白 con + fess = together + speak

108.fid

表达语义：trust

例词：

fidelity：诚实；真实 fid + elity = trust + elity（名词后缀）

109.fict

表达语义：feign（变化型：fig）

例词：

fictive：虚构的 fict + ive = feign + ive（形容词后缀）

110.fil

表达语义：thread；spin（变化型；fila）

例词：

filament：细丝；细线 fila + ment = thread + ment（名词后缀）

111.fin

表达语义：end

例词：

final：最终的 fin + al = end + al（形容词后缀）

112.flat

表达语义：blow

例词：

inflate：膨胀；通胀 in + flate = in + blow

113.flect

表达语义：bend（变化型：flex）

例词：

reflect：折射 re + flect = back + bend

114.flu

表达语义：flow

例词：

fluent：流利的 flu + ent = flow + ent（此处为形容词后缀）

fluctuate：起伏 flu + ctu + ate = flow + ctu + ate（此处为动词后缀）

confluent：汇集 con + flu + ent = together + flow + ent（此处为形容词后缀）

115.fract

表达语义：break（变化型：frag）

例词：

fracture：折断；骨折 fract + ure = break + ure（名词后缀）

116.fuse

表达语义：pour（变化型：found）

例词：

confuse：混乱；迷惑 con + fuse = together + pour

117.gene（r）

表达语义：produce；race

例词：

genealogy：宗谱 gene + alogy = produce + study（名词后缀）

genesis：开端 gene + sis = produce + sis（名词后缀）

118.geo

表达语义：earth

例词：

geology：地质学 geo + logy = earth + study

119.ger

表达语义：carry（变化型：gest）

例词：

exaggerate：夸大 ex + ag +ger + ate = out + to + carry + ate（此处为动词后缀）

120.greg

表达语义：flock；herd

例词：

aggregate：聚集 ag + greg + ate = to + flock + ate（此处为动词后缀）

121.grad

表达语义：walk（变化型：gress）

例词：

gradual：逐渐地 grad + ual = walk + ual（形容词后缀）

122.gram/graph

表达语义：write

例词：

epigram：警句 epi + gram = on + write

123.grat

表达语义：please

例词：

gratuity：赠物；赏钱 grat + uity = please + uity（名词后缀）

124.grav

表达语义：heavy

例词：

gravity：重力 grav + ity = heavy + ity（名词后缀）

125.hap

表达语义：luck

例词：

perhaps：可能的 per + hap = through + luck

haphazard：偶然性；偶然的 hap + hazard = luck + hazard

126.helio

表达语义：sun

例词：

heliocentric：日心的 helio + centric = sun + center

heliotherapy：日光疗法 helio + therapy = sun + therapy

127.here

表达语义：stick（变化型：hes）

例词：

inhesion：内在；天赋 in + hes + ion = in + stick + ion（名词后缀）

cohesive：黏合在一起 co + hes + ive = together + stick + ive（形容词后缀）

128.hum

表达语义：man；ground（变化型：hom）

例词：

homicide：谋杀 hom + cide = man + kill

exhume：发掘 ex + hum = out + ground

129.idio

表达语义：personal；distinct

例词：

idiopathic：自发；原发的 idio + path + ic = personal + disease + ic（形容词后缀）

130.insul

表达语义：island

例词：

insulation：绝缘；隔离 insul + ation = island + ation（名词后缀）

131.it

表达语义：go

例词：

ambit：周围；范围 amb +-it = around + go

132.ject

表达语义：throw（变化型：jac）

例词：

ejaculate：突然说出；射出 e + jac + ulate = out + throw + ul + ate（此处为动词后缀）

133.labor

表达语义：work

例词：

collaborate：合作 col + labor + ate = together + work + ate（此处为动词后缀）

elaborate：仔细说明 e + labor + ate = out + work + ate（此处为动词后缀）

134.laps

表达语义：slip；glide；fall

例词：

collapse：崩溃 col + lapse = together + fall

elapse：流逝 e + lapse = out + slip

relapse：复发 re + lapse = back + fall

135.late

表达语义：bring；carry

例词：

ablation：腐蚀；切除 ab + lat + ion = away + carry + ion（名词后缀）

translate：翻译 trans + late = across + carry

136.later

表达语义：side

例词：

lateral：侧面；旁边的 later + al = side + al（此处为形容词后缀）

collateral：并行的；附随的 col + later + al = with side + al（此处为形容词后缀）

137.lav

表达语义：wash（变化型：lau）

例词：

lava：熔岩 lav + a = wash + a（名词后缀）

138.lax

表达语义：loosen（变化型：lyse）

例词：

laxity：松弛；不检点 lax + ity = loosen + ity（名词后缀）

paralysis：瘫痪 para + lys + is = side + loosen + is（名词后缀）

139.lect

表达语义：choose；gather；read（变化型：leg）

例词：

collect：收集 col + lect = together + gather

140.leg

表达语义：appoint；send

例词：

legator：遗赠者 leg + ator = appoint + ator（名词后缀）

relegate：驱逐；降低地位 re + leg + ate = back + appoint + ate（此处为动词后缀）

141.lev

表达语义：raise；light

例词：

levitate：轻轻浮起；漂浮 lev + it + ate = raise + go + ate（此处为动词后缀）

142.liber

表达语义：free

例词：

liberal：自由；不拘泥的 liber + al = free + al（形容词后缀）

143.libr

表达语义：book（变化型：lib）

例词：

libretto：歌词集；剧本 libre + tto = book + tto（名词后缀）

144.lic

表达语义：permit

例词：

illicit：违法的 il + lic + it = not + permit + it（名词后缀）

145.lig

表达语义：bind

例词：

ligate：结扎；绑扎 lig + ate = bind + ate（此处为动词后缀）

obligate：负有责任 ob + lig + ate = to + bind + ate（此处为

动词后缀）

146.liter

表达语义：letter

例词：

literal：文字的 liter + al = letter + al（形容词后缀）

illiterate：文盲 il + liter + ate = not + letter + ate（此处为形容词后缀）

preliterate：增殖；扩散 pre + liter + ate = before + letter + ate（此处为形容词后缀）

transliterate：直译 trans + liter + ate = across + letter + ate（此处为动词后缀）

147.log

表达语义：speech（变化型：loq）

例词：

epilogue：结语 epi + logue = in addition + speech

eulogy：颂词 eu + log + y = good + speech + y（名词后缀）

neology：新词 neo + log + y = new + speech + y（名词后缀）

eloquence：口才 e + loqu + ence = out speech + ence（名词后缀）

148.lud

表达语义：play

例词：

collude：勾结；串通 col + lude = together + play

149.lust

表达语义：bright；illuminate（变化型：luc）

例词：

lucent：透明；光亮的 luc + ent = bright + ent（此处为形容词后缀）

illustrate：解释；注释 in + lust + rate = upon + illuminate + ate（此处为动词后缀）

lustrous：有光泽的 lust + rous = bright + rous（形容词后缀）

150.man

表达语义：hand（变化型：manu）

例词：

manufacture：制造 manu + fact + ure = hand + make + ure（名词后缀）

151.mand

表达语义：order；entrust（变化型：mend）

例词：

mandator：命令者；托管人 mand + ator = order + tor（名词）

152.medi

表达语义：middle

例词：

mediacy：调节；媒介 medi + acy = middle + acy（名词后缀）

153.ment

表达语义：think；mind

例词：

mental：大脑的；精神的 ment + al = mind + al（此处为形容词后缀）

154.merc（h）

表达语义：trade；reward

例词：

Merchant：商人 merch + ant = trade + ant（此处为名词后缀）

155.min

表达语义：jut；project

例词：

preeminence：卓越；杰出 pre + e + min + ence = before + out + jut + ence（名词后缀）

156.min

表达语义：small

例词：

minute：分钟；微小 min + ute = small + ute

157.mir

表达语义：wonder；behold；reflect（变化型：mar）

例词：

mirage：幻景 mir + age = wonder + age（名词后缀）

marvel：感到惊奇 mar + vel = wonder + el

158.miss

表达语义：send；throw（变化型：mit）

例词：

Transmit：传递；传送 trans + mit = across + send

159.mon

表达语义：advise；remind

例词：

admonitory：劝告；训诫 ad + mon + itory = to + advise + itory（此处为形容词后缀）

160.morph

表达语义：form

例词：

morphology：形态学；词法 morph + ology = form + study

161.mort

表达语义：death

例词：

mortality：死亡 mort + ality = death + ality（名词后缀）

162.mount

表达语义：ascend

例词：

mountable：可登上的 mount + able = ascend + able（形容词后缀）

163.mov

表达语义：move（变化型：mob；mot）

例词：

motivate：驱动刺激 mot + iv + ate = move + iv + ate（此处为动词后缀）

164.muni

表达语义：service；gift

例词：

munificence：丰厚；慷慨给予 muni + fic + cence = service + do + ence（名词后缀）

165.mut

表达语义：change

例词：

mutability：易变性 mut + ability = change + ability（名词后缀）

166.nat

表达语义：born

例词：

agnate：男方亲属 ag + nate = to + born

cognate：同族；同语系的 cog + nate = together + born

postnatal：产后 post + nat + al = after + born + al（此处为形容词后缀）

prenatal：产前的 pre + nat + al = before + born + al（此处为形容词后缀）

neonate：新生儿 neo + nate = new + born

167.necro

表达语义：death

例词：

necrology：死者名册；讣告 necro + ology = death + speak

necropolis：大墓地 necro + polis = death + city

168.nect

表达语义：bind（变化型：nex）

例词：

Annex：附加物；附属建筑 an + nex = to bind

nexus：连接；关系 nex + us = bind + us（名词后缀）

169.neg

表达语义：deny；not

例词：

negate：否定；否认 neg + ate = deny + ate（此处为动词后缀）

neglect：忽视 neg + lect = not + choose

abnegate：放弃；舍弃 ab + neg + ate = away + deny + ate（此处为动词后缀）

170.neur

表达语义：nerve（变化型：neuron；nerv）

例词：

neuritis：神经炎 neur + itis = nerve + ill

neurosis：神经症 neur + osis = nerve + osis（名词后缀）

enervate：使衰弱 e + nerv + ate = out + nerve + ate（此处为动词后）

171.neutr

表达语义：neither

例词：

neutrality：中立 neutr + ality = neither + ality（名词后缀）

172.noc

表达语义：harm（变化型：nox）

例词：

nocuous：有毒的 noc + uous = harm + uous（形容词后缀）

innocence：无辜 in + noc + cence = no + harm + ence（名词后缀）

173.noct

表达语义：night（变化型：nox）

例词：

noctambulism：夜游 noct + ambul + ism = night + walk + ism（名词后缀）

equinox：春秋分 equi + nox = equal + night

174.nomin

表达语义：name（变化型：nom）

例词：

denominate：用指定货币单位结算 de + nomin + ate = down + name + ate（此处为动词后缀）

175.norm

表达语义：rule

例词：

enormity：暴行；极恶 e + norm + ity = out + rule + ity（名词后缀）

176.not

表达语义：mark

例词：

notation：符号；注释；评注 not + ation = mark + ation（名词后缀）

177.nounce

表达语义：report（变化型：nunci）

例词：

Annunciate：宣告 an + nunci + ate = to + report + ate（此处为动词后缀）

178.nov

表达语义：new

例词：

novice：新手 nov + ice = new + ice（名词后缀）

179.ocul

表达语义：eye

例词：

oculist：眼科专家 ocul + ist = eye + ist（名词后缀）

180.onym

表达语义：name

例词：

anonymous：匿名 an + onym + out = no + name + ous（形容词后缀）

pseudonym：假名 pseud + nym = false + name

181.oper

表达语义：work

例词：

operation：操作；运营 oper + ation = work + ation（名词后缀）

182.opt

表达语义：wish

例词：

optimum：最佳效果 opt + mum = wish + m + um（名词后缀）

183.opt

表达语义：sight；eye

例词：

optometer：验光仪 opt + meter = sight + measure

184.ora

表达语义：speak

例词：

oration：演说 ora + tion = speak + tion（名词后缀）

185.ori

表达语义：rise；begin（变化型：orig）

例词：

origin：起源 orig + in = begin + in（名词后缀）

186.orn

表达语义：decorate；furnish

例词：

ornament：装饰 orn + a + ment = decorate + ment（名词后缀）

187.ortho

表达语义：straight；right

例词：

orthodox：ortho + dox = right + opinion

188.oss

表达语义：bone（变化型：osteo）

例词：

ossification：骨化 oss + ifi + cation = bone + ify + cation（名词后缀）

189.pact

表达语义：agree；fasten

例词：

compact：压缩 com + pact + together + fasten

190.pan

表达语义：all

例词：

panacea：万能药 pan +ac + ea = all + healing + ea（名词后缀）

191.passi

表达语义：suffer；feelings（变化型：pati；path）

例词：

sympathy：同情 sym + path + y = same + feeling + y（名词后缀）

pathology：病理学 path + ology = suffering + study

192.ped

表达语义：foot；child

例词：

pedestrian：步行的人 ped + estr + ian = foot + stand + ian（名词后缀）

193.pel

表达语义：drive（变化型：puls）

例词：

compel：强迫 com + pel = together + drive

impulse：冲动 im + pulse = in + drive

194.pen

表达语义：punish（变化型：pun）

例词：

penalty：刑罚 pen + al + ty = punish + al + ty（名词后缀）

195.pend

表达语义：hang；weigh（变化型：pens）

例词：

appendix：附录；阑尾 ap + pend + ix = to + hang + ix（名词后缀）

compendium：概要；概略 com + pen + ium = together + hang + ium（名词后缀）

expend：耗尽 spend or use up resources（as money，time，energy）

196.pet

表达语义：fly；seek

例词：

petition：请愿 pet + ti + tion = seek + ti + tion（名词后缀）

197.phil

表达语义：love

例词：

philanthropist：慈善家 phil + anthrop + ist = love + human + ist（名词后缀）

198.phobia

表达语义：fear

例词：

acrophobia：恐高症 acro + phobia = high + fear

199.phon

表达语义：sound（变化型：phe）

例词：

prophecy：预言 pro + phe + cy = forward + sound + cy（名词后缀）

200.pict

表达语义：paint；picture

例词：

depict：描绘；表现 de + pict = down + paint

201.plac

表达语义：please（变化型：pleas）

例词：

placate：平息；安抚 plac + ate = please + ate（此处为动词后缀）

complacent：自满 com + plac + ent = with + please + ent（此处为形容词后缀）

202.plen

表达语义：fill；full（变化型：plete；ple；pli；ply）

例词：

plenary：全体参加的 plen + ary = full + ary（形容词后缀）

amplify：扩音；增强 am + pli + fy = around + fill + ify（动词后缀）

supply：供应；提供 su + ply = below + fill

203.ply

表达语义：fold（变化型：pli；ple）

例词：

plywood：夹板 ply + wood = fold + wood

204.polis

表达语义：city

例词：

acropolis：卫城 acro + polis = high + city

205.pon

表达语义：put（变化型：pound）

例词：

compound：合成 com + pound = together + put

206.popul

表达语义：people（变化型：publ）

例词：

population：人口 popul + ation = people + ation（名词后缀）

207.port

表达语义：carry；gate

例词：

portable：便携的 port + able = carry + able（形容词后缀）

transport：运输 trans + port = across + gate

208.pos

表达语义：put；place

例词：

impose：强加 im + pose = in + put

propose：提议 pro + pose = forward + put

209.potent

表达语义：power

例词：

potential：可能；有潜力的 potent + ial = power + ial（此处为形容词后缀）

210.preci

表达语义：price

例词：

depreciation：贬值 de + preci + ation = down + price + ation

（名词后缀）

211.prim

表达语义：first（变化型：prin；prem）

例词：

primitive：远古；早期的 prim + mit + ive = first + send + ive（形容词后缀）

212.pris

表达语义：seize（变化型：prehend）

例词：

comprehend：理解 com + prehend = together + seize

prison：监狱 pris + on = seize + on（名词后缀）

213.proach

表达语义：near（变化型：proxim）

例词：

approach：接近 ap + proach = to near

proximity：附近 proxim + ity = near + ity（名词后缀）

214.prob

表达语义：test；try；examine（变化型：prov）

例词：

probable：可能 prob + able = test + able（形容词后缀）

215.psych

表达语义：soul；mind

例词：

psychology：心理学 psych + ology = mind + study

216.purg

表达语义：purify

例词：

purgative：净化的；赎罪的 purg + ative = purify + ative（形容词后缀）

217.pute

表达语义：think

例词：

putative：公认的 put + ative = think + ative（形容词后缀）

repute：被普遍认为 re + pute = repeat + think

218.qui

表达语义：calm；rest

例词：

tranquility：tran + qui + lity = across + calm + lity（名词后缀）

219.quire

表达语义：seek（变化型：quisit；quest）

例词：

acquire：获得 ac + quire = to + seek

220.rad

表达语义：scrape（变化型：ras）

例词：

erase：抹去；擦掉 e + ras = out + scrape

221.radic

表达语义：root

例词：

radiation：放射；辐射 radi + ation = root + ation（名词后缀）

radical：激进的 radic + al = root + al（此处为形容词后缀）

222.rap

表达语义：snatch（变化型：rav）

例词：

ravage：彻底毁灭 rav + age = snatch + age（名词后缀）

223.rat

表达语义：reckon；reason（变型：ratio）

例词：

ratify：正式批准 rat + ify = reckon + ify（动词后缀）

rational：合理的 rat + ion + al = reason + ion + al（此处为形容词后缀）

224.rect

表达语义：right；straight

例词：

rectify：矫正 rect + ify = right + ify（动词后缀）

225.reg

表达语义：rule

例词：

regal：帝王的 reg + al = rule + al（此处为形容词后缀）

226.rog

表达语义：ask

例词：

interrogative：疑问；讯问 inter + rog + ative = between + ask + ative（形容词后缀）

227.rud

表达语义：raw

例词：

rudiment：原理 rudi + ment = raw + ment（名词后缀）

228.rupt

表达语义：break

例词：

erupt：爆发 e + rupt = out + break

229.sal

表达语义：salt；leap（变化型 sult）

例词：

salient：最重要；最突出的 sal + ient = salt + ent（此处为形容词后缀）

230.sat

表达语义：full（变化型：satur）

例词：

satiation：满足 sat + ation = full + ation（名词后缀）

saturate：饱和 satur + ate = full + ate（此处为动词后缀）

231.sci

表达语义：know

例词：

conscience：良知 con + sci + ence = with + know + ence（名词后缀）

nescience：无知 ne + sci + ent = not + know + ence（名词后缀）

232.scribe

表达语义：write（变化型：script）

例词：

circumscribe：约束 circum + scribe = around + write

inscribe：铭记；题写 in + scribe = in + write

postscript：附言 post + script = after + write

233.sect

表达语义：cut

例词：

intersect：横穿；贯穿 inter + sect = between + cut

transect：横切 trans + sect = across + cut

234.sed

表达语义：sit（变化：sess；sid）

例词：

sediment：沉淀物 sedi + ment = sit + ment（名词后缀）

assess：估价 as + sess = to sit

dissidence：持不同政见 dis + sid + ence = apart + sit + ence
（名词后缀）

235.sequ

表达语义：follow（变化：secut；su）

例词：

sequence：顺序 sequ + ence = follow + ence（名词后缀）

236.sert

表达语义：join；put

例词：

assertion：断言；主张 as + sert + ion = to + put + ion（名词
后缀）

237.sign

表达语义：mark

例词：

signify：象征；预示 sign + ify = mark + ify（动词后缀）

design：设计 de + sign = down + mark

238.sist

表达语义：stand（变化：stitut；sta；st）

例词：

persistent：坚持；持续的 per + sist + ent = thoroughly + stand + ent（此处为形容词后缀）

subsist：供养 sub + sist = under + stand

destitute：穷困的 de + statute = down + stand

resistive：抗……的 re + sist + ive = back + stand +ive（形容词后缀）

distant：远的 di + st + ant = away + stand +ant（此处为形容词后缀）

239.sol

表达语义：alone

例词：

solitude：孤独；独居 sol + itude = alone + itude（名词后缀）

console：安慰 con + sole = with + alone

240.solv

表达语义：loosen（变化型：solut）

例词：

solvent：溶剂 solv + ent = loosen + ent（此处为名词后缀）

241.somn

表达语义：sleep

例词：

insomnia：失眠 in + somn + ia = not + sleep + ia（名词后缀）

242.son

表达语义：sound

例词：

resonance：（声音）圆润, 低沉, 饱满 re + son + ance = back + sound + ance（名词后缀）

243.soph

表达语义：wise；wisdom

例词：

philosophy：哲学 philo + soph + y = love + wisdom + y（此

处为名词后缀）

244.sort

表达语义：kind

例词：

assortment：各种各样的人或物 as + sort + ment = to + kind + ment（名词后缀）

resort：再分类 re + sort = back + kind

245.spec

表达语义：see；look

例词：

prospect：前景 pro + spect = forward + look

246.sper

表达语义：hope

例词：

desperate：绝望 de + sper + ate = down + hope + ate（此处为形容词后缀）

247.spers

表达语义：scatter

例词：

dispersal：分散 dis + pers + al = away + scatter + al（此处为名词后缀）

248.sphere

表达语义：ball

例词：

hemisphere：半球 hemi + sphere = half + ball

249.spir

表达语义：breathe

例词：

inspiration：灵感 in + spir + ation = in + breathe + ation（名词后缀）

250.stru；struct

表达语义：build

例词：

instruct：指示 in + struct = in + build

instrumental：作为手段的 in + stru + ment + al = in + build + ment + al（此处为形容词后缀）

251.surge

表达语义：rise（变化型：surrect）

例词：

resurgence：复活 re + surge + ence = back + rise + ence（名词后缀）

252.tac

表达语义：silent

例词：

tacit：不言而喻的 tac + it = quiet + go

253.tail

表达语义：cut

例词：

detail：细节 de + tail = down + cut

entail：使成为必需或必然 en + tail = in + cut

retail：零售 re + tail = repeat + cut

254.tang

表达语义：touch（变化：tact；tag）

例词：

tangible：触知的 tang + ible = change + ible（形容词后缀）

255.tain

表达语义：hold；keep（变化型：ten；tin）

例词：

appertain：关于；涉及 ap + per + tain = to + thorough + hold

tenure：享有；保有期 ten + ure = hold + ure（名词后缀）

256.tect

表达语义：cover（变化：sembl）

例词：

protect：保护 pro + tect = forward + cover

257.tend

表达语义：stretch（变化：tent；tens）

例词：

tendon：筋 tend + on = stretch + on（名词后缀）

258.term

表达语义：boundary

例词：

terminate：终结 term + in + ate = boundary + in + ate（此处为动词后缀）

259.test

表达语义：witness

例词：

attestation：证明 at + test + ation = to + witness + ation（名词后缀）

260.text

表达语义：weave

例词：

texture：质地；肌理 text + ure = weave + ure（名词后缀）

261.the；theo

表达语义：god

例词：

atheist：无神论者 a + the + ist = no + god + ist（名词后缀）

262.tort

表达语义：twist

例词：

torture：折磨，刑讯 tort + ure = twist + ure（名词后缀）

contort：扭曲 con + tort = together + twist

extort：讹诈 ex + tort = out + twist

retort：反驳 re + tort = back + twist

263.tract

表达语义：draw（变化：treat）

例词：

protract：延长；拖延 pro + tract = forward + draw

264.tribute

表达语义：pay；bestow

例词：

attribute：把……归于 at + tribute = to + pay

265.trus

表达语义：thrust（变化型：trude）

例词：

extrusive：突出的 ex + trus + ive = out + thrust + ive（形容词后缀）

266.turb

表达语义：disturb

例词：

perturb：扰乱；烦恼 per + turb = thorough + disturb

267.us

表达语义：use（变化型：uti）

例词：

utilize：使用；利用 uti + lize = use + l + ize（动词后缀）

268.vac/van；void

表达语义：empty（变化型：van；void）

例词：

vanish：消失 van + ish = empty + ish（此处为动词后缀）

269.vade

表达语义：go（变化：wade）

例词：

pervade：弥漫；流行 per + vade = thoroughly + go

270.vaga

表达语义：wander

例词：

divagate：离题 di + vaga + ate = apart + wander + ate（此处为动词后缀）

271.val

表达语义：strong；worth（变化型：vail）

例词：

valor：勇气；勇敢 val + or = strong + or（名词后缀）

272.ven

表达语义：come（变化型：vent）

例词：

circumvent：绕行；陷害 circum + vent = around + come

273.ver

表达语义：true

例词：

verity：真实；真理 ver + ity = true + ity（名词后缀）

274.verb

表达语义：word

例词：

verbal：与语言有关 verb + al = word + al（此处为动词后缀）

275.verg

表达语义：to incline

例词：

converge：汇合 con + verge = together + incline

276.vers

表达语义：to turn（变化型：vert）

例词：

adverse：不利的 ad + verse = to + turn

277.vi

表达语义：way（变化型：voy）

例词：

viaduct：高架路 via + duct = way + lead

deviate：偏离 de + vi + ate = apart + way + ate（此处为动词后缀）

278.viv

表达语义：to live

例词：

revive：复活；重兴 re + viv = back + live

279. vita

表达语义：life

例词：

revitalize：振兴 re + vita + lize = back + life + ize（动词后缀）

280. voc；voke

表达语义：to call；voice（变化型：voke）

例词：

vocalist：歌者 voc + al + ist = voice + al + ist（名词后缀）

281. volve；volut

表达语义：to roll

例词：

revolver：左轮手枪 re + volv + er = repeat + roll + er（名词后缀）

282. vor

表达语义：to eat

例词：

carnivore：肉食动物 carn + vore = meat + eat

第三节　构词成分

构词成分（combining form）是一种构词形式（大家可以理解为类似汉字笔画），和词根词缀一样，构词成分也经常出现在不同的单词中，具有重复性，因此掌握常用的构词成分会帮助我们高效地记忆和使用词汇，甚至可以帮助我们猜出生词的大概含义。以下为笔者收集整理的构词成分供大家参考：

epi-：在……之上，或表面 epilogue 结语

-fest：节日 jazzfest talkfest 等

geo：与地球有关的 geology 地质学

gon：角 hexagon 六角形

-geny：发展或发生 organogeny

-lithic：stone Paleolithic 旧石器的

-graph："写"或"画"的东西 pictograph 象形文字

-graphy：描述性科学 geography（写、画）的风格,（某主题）的描述

gyneco-：与女性有关 gynecology 妇科学

gyro-：回旋的 gyrocopter 自转旋翼飞机

haem-：与血有关 hematology 血液学

-hedron：……面体 hexahedron 六面体

helio-：与太阳有关的 heliocentric 日心说

hepatic-：与肝有关 hepatitis 肝炎

hepta-：七 heptagon 七角形

hetero-：别的,不同的(与 homo 相对) heterosexism 异性恋

Hexa-：六 hexameter 六音步

hind-：后面的 hind-limb 后肢

holo－：全面的 holography 全息摄影

-hood：状态；特性；集合 childhood 童年

hydro-：与水有关 hydropower 水电

hyper-：超常的 hyperactive 亢奋, hypergamy 高攀婚姻

hypo-：低于正常的；与上一个相反 hypoallergic 低过敏性的

idio-：自己的；个人的 idiotype 个体基因型 idiolect 个人语言

kine-：运动的 kinetic energy 物理动能

lact-：与"乳"有关 lactarium 乳制品店

-laden：充满…… fruit-laden 硕果累累的

leuco-：白的 leucotomy 脑白质切断术

ligno-：与木有关 lignocellulose 木纤维素

-liner：表示……行字的讲话等 15-liner 15 行

lipo-：与脂肪有关的 lipogenesis 脂肪生成, lipoma 脂肪瘤

litho-：与石有关,与结石有关 lithology 岩石学

-logue：表说话或编写 epilogue 结语, dialogue 对话

lymph-：与淋巴有关的 lymphoma 淋巴癌

-lysis：分解；反应物 paralysis 麻痹症

macro-：长的；大的 macroscopic 宏观的

mal-：不好的 malfunction 故障

-mancy：表占卜；语言 geomancy 泥土占卜

-mania：……狂，……癖 bookmania 读书狂

maxi-：特大；特长的 maximum 最大的

mega-：巨大的 megacity 巨型城市

-mer：表聚合物和分子 polymer 聚合物

meso-：表中间的 mesomorph 中型体型的

meta-：（met- 在原音前）表变化、变位 metamorphosis 质变

-meter：计仪表 barometer 压力表

micro：微小的 microphone 麦克风

md-：……中间的 midway 中途

milli-：表千分之，毫…… milliliter 毫升

mini-：小型的 miniskirt 超短裙

mon-：单一的（在元音前，同 mono）monarch 君主

-monger：贩子 warmonger 战争贩子

mono-：单一 monolingual 单一语言

-mony：动作；状态；品质 hegemony 霸权主义

-morph：形态；特征 mesomorph 中型体型

-most：最……的 southernmost 最南边的

multi-：多…… multilateral 多边的

must-：必须……的 must-have 必备的

myco-：真菌的 mycoprotein 菌蛋白

-mycin：霉素 erythromycin 红霉素

myo-：表肌肉 myocardium 心肌

nano-：毫微的 nanometer 纳米

narco-：昏迷状态 narco-terrorism 毒品恐怖主义

naso-：与鼻子有关的 naso-gastric 鼻饲的

necro-：死或尸体 necrosis 坏死

nega-：表负的 negation 否定

neo-：新的 Neolithic 新石器的

nephro-：肾的 nephrosis 肾病

neuro-：与神经有关的 neurological 神经病学的

noct-：与"夜"有关 nocturnal 夜间发生的

-nomy："学""法" astronomy 天文学

nona-：与 9 有关 nonagon nonagenarian 90 ~ 99 的人

oct-：表 8 …… octopus 八爪鱼

oligo-：少数；少量的 oligotrophic（湖泊等）少营养的

-ology：学科；学说 neurology 神经学

-oma：表肿瘤 carcinoma 癌

omni-：全；全部 omnipresent 无处不在

onco-：肿瘤的 oncology 肿瘤学

-onym：名称；词 pseudonym 化名

-orium：场馆等特殊场所 auditorium 学术报告厅

ortho-：正的；直的 orthography 正字学

-osis：表过程、状态、病变状态 neurosis 神经症 thrombosis

osteo-：与"骨"有关 osteogenesis 骨生成

oto-：与"耳"有关 otology 耳科学

paedo-：与儿童有关 pedophile 恋童癖

-oid：表类别，表外形 Negroid 尼戈鲁人

palaeo-：（paleo 北美）古的；原始的 Paleolithic 旧石器时代

pan-：全；总的；泛 panorama 全景画

panto-：全部，表意动作 panto 哑剧

patho-：与病有关的 pathology 病理学

-pathy：感情；感觉 empathy 同情

per-：完全的，穿过，毁坏 perceive 理解

peri-：周围；环绕 pericardium 心包 perimeter 周边

perma-：永久的 permanent 永恒的

petro-：与岩石有关的，与石油有关的 petroleum 石油

pheno-：显出；表现 phenomena 现象

-phile：喜爱……的 bibliophile 藏书家

-philia：……癖好 pedophilia 恋童症

philo-：爱……；亲……philopatric 回家冲动 philosophy 哲
学（love of wisdom）

-phobe：恐……的人 homophobe 憎恨同性恋的人 xenophobe
排外或害怕生人的人

-phobia：恐…… acrophobia 恐高症

-phone：传音装置 megaphone 说……语言的人 anglophone

说英语的人 francophone 说法语的人

phospho-：与磷有关 phospholipid 磷脂

photo-：与光有关，与照相有关 photobiology 光生物学

phyto-：与植物有关的 phytogeography 植物地理学

-plegia：某种瘫痪 hemiplegia 偏瘫，paraplegia 截瘫

poly-：聚合；多 polyster 聚酯

physio-：自然地 physiognomy 观相学

preter-：超；多于 preternatural 超自然的

pro-：亲；支持 pro-west 亲西方的

proto-：最早的；原始的 prototype 原型

pseudo-：伪；假的 pseudonym 化名

pyro-：与"火"有关的 pyrogen 热源

quasi-：貌似；准……；类似 quasi-military 准军事性的

radio-：无线电的，射线的 radiobiology 放射生物学

reti- retic-：网的 retina 视网膜

retro-：向后；回报 retrospect 回顾

rhino-：与鼻子有关的 rhinoplasty 鼻整容术

rhizo-：与"根"有关的 rhizome 根茎

-saur：（已灭绝的）爬行动物 dinosaur 恐龙

-scape：特定的景色 moonscape 月景

schizo-：分裂的 schizogony 裂殖生殖 schizoid 似精神分裂的

-seater：表车、沙发、建筑有……座位的 seven-seater 七座车

seleno-：与月亮有关的 selenology 月球学

self-：自我……的 self-taught 自学的

sero-：血清的 serodiagnose 血清诊断

Sexi-：六的 sexivalent 六价的

sino-：中国的 sino-Japanese relationship 中日关系

socio-：社会的 sociobiology 社会生物学

sono-：与声音有关的 Sonometer 超声波计

-speak：×× 行业的行话

-sphere：球体的，尤指环绕地球的地区 atmosphere 大气层

uni-：单独 unilateral 单边的

第四节　英文词缀

在充分地了解了词根和构词成分之后，我们来看看相对比较容易掌握的词缀（affix）。词缀分前缀（prefix）和后缀（suffix）。前缀更多地帮助改变词义，而后缀更多地帮助改变词性，但两者也都有另外的功能。以下为英文中比较常用的词缀：

age：shortage marriage leakage drainage
al：denial betrayal dismissal withdrawal
an：American Russian Asian African
ance：attendance guidance performance assistance
ant：applicant consultant participant
ary：dictionary missionary boundary commentary
ate：doctorate consulate electorate directorate
ation：examination education decoration temptation
cy：accuracy efficiency privacy bureaucracy
dom：freedom kingdom wisdom boredom
ee：employee absentee refugee trustee
eer：engineer mountaineer auctioneer profiteer
ence：difference existence preference diligence
er：writer trainer teacher
ery：bribery embroidery mockery machinery
ese：Chinese Japanese
ess：actress princess goddess hostess
ful：handful spoonful bagful busful
hood：childhood motherhood knighthood
ian：magician musician historian mathematician
ing：shopping feeling reading sightseeing
ion：action decision collection creation
ism/ist：socialism socialist
ity：prosperity equality formality majority

let：piglet booklet starlet bracelet playlet
ment：endorsement investment
ness：happiness sadness weakness bitterness
or：actor
ry：jewelry slavery bravery bribery
ship：ownership sportsmanship entrepreneurship
ty：loyalty safety cruelty penalty
ure：failure pleasure departure pressure
y：modesty difficulty discovery inquiry
arian：librarian vegetarian humanitarian

suffix（adjective）

ible：permissible negligible collapsible
able：valuable lovable miserable
al：cultural logical
ant：important
ary：momentary imaginary
ate：fortunate affectionate passionate
en：woolen wooden golden
ent：different
ful：beautiful hopeful cheerful
ic：realistic poetic historic
ical：classical geographical
ish：childish selfish foolish
ive：active effective
ly：friendly costly orderly
ous：courageous furious nervous

suffix（verb）

ate	activate	originate	motivate	hyphenate
en	widen	sharpen	brighten	sweeten
ify	simplify	purify	notify	justify
ize	apologize	emphasize	criticize	

prefix prefix to change part of speech

a- add to nouns to form adj or adv asleep aboard aside ashore ablaze
be- add to noun or adj. to form verb befriend belittle bewitch behead bedim
em- add to nouns to form verbs embark embed embody empower embitter
en- add to nouns or adj to form verbs endanger encourage enrage enforce enslave enrich enlarge ennoble endear enable
out- add to nouns or adj to form verbs outnumber outpace outwit

　　以上三种形式的组词法可以帮助我们高效地掌握单词,了解单词的构成特点,也能帮助我们准确使用单词。

第五节　分类应用

　　在扩大了单词量的基础上,我们还应该知道怎样准确地使用单词和表达法,而对单词的深度理解是准确运用的基础。笔者将一些单词和表达法进行了分类:委婉(euphemism)、褒义(approving)、贬义(derogatory)、比喻(figurative)、肢体语言、外来语、古语、称谓、正式与非正式语、同近义词。目的是为大家提供单词储备,帮助大家对单词实现多角度理解,最终运用到翻译实践中去。

一、委婉用词

　　英语国家的文化特点决定了其在表达有关个人隐私和一些敏感事物上,多会采用委婉说法,翻译时注意委婉用语的使用,不仅彰显译者的语言功力,可体现为人教养。下面是一些委婉表达及用词例子。

bathroom/restroom/washroom 卫生间

go to lavatory 如厕

Ordure 排泄物

Memory garden 墓地

Rest 入土

Eternal peace/pass away 死亡

Physically disadvantaged 残疾人

Senior citizen 老年人

African American 美国黑人

Economically disadvantaged 困难人群

Unwaged 无工资或固定收入的人

Meat technologist 屠夫

Sanitary engineer 清洁工

Overweight 肥胖

Expecting 怀孕

Waterworks 人体泌尿系统（的功能）

Strong language 脏话

Professional foul 故意犯规

Untrue 撒谎

Sticky finger 小偷小摸

Be no better than she should be（性关系随便）

Born on wrong side of the blanket 私生子

二、褒义词

褒义词的正确使用也是极其重要的。中国俗语："人人爱听拜年话！"可见"夸赞"是人际交往中必不可少的语言艺术。因此，掌握一些褒义词并恰当使用，会产生很好的社交效果。那么作为翻译人员，更加需要这样的词汇来精准传神地传达说话人或作者的用意。以下为一些常用褒义词的例词。

Ladylike：like or suitable for a lady；polite；dignified 淑女般的

Becoming: of dress suitable to the wearer, appropriate 着装得体的

Breeding: good manner because of training or family background 有教养的

Character: man who's not ordinary or typical 人物

Clean-limbed: having well-formed slender limbs 修长的四肢

Consistence: 一致性；一贯性

Constancy: quality of being firm and unchanged 坚定的

Cosmopolitan: free from national prejudice because of wide experience of the world 见多识广

Craggy: 五官轮廓分明

Curious: eager to know or learn 好学的

Foxy: (of a woman) physically attractive and sexy 性感的

Funky: very modern and fashionable 时尚的

Gentility: genteel manners and behavior; social superiority 高贵

Homey: like home; cozy 温暖如家一般

Immaculate: perfectly clean and tidy; spotless 一尘不染

Intelligentsia: 知识阶层

Leading light: 领军人物

Mouthwatering: 美味

Novel: new and strange 新颖

Peaches and cream: having an attractive pink color 甜美可爱

Persevere with sth.: continue doing sth. in spite of difficulties 坚持不懈

Petite: (of a girl or woman) having a small and dainty physique 小巧

Poetic: like or suggesting poetry, esp. in being graceful and aesthetically leasing 诗情画意

Polymath: person who knows a great deal about many different subjects 知识渊博的人

Pristine: fresh and clean, as if new 新鲜的

Professionalism: quality skill of a profession or its member 有层次的

Proven: that has been tested and demonstrated 真正的

Provident: having or showing wisdom for future needs 有先见之明

Sophisticated: good education and manner 有修养的

Unimpeachable: that can not be questioned or doubted 毫无疑问

Unpretentious: not showy or pompous 真诚

Untiring: 不知疲倦

Towering/outstanding 杰出的

三、贬义词

贬义词虽然没有褒义词那么讨喜,却也是非常重要的一类词汇,在很多场合当我们表达不满或遗憾的时候,准确地使用这些贬义词,能很好地表达我们内心的微妙活动。当然,我们需要更加谨慎地使用这些词汇,以避免一些麻烦。下面是一些常用贬义词的例词。

La-di-da 做作的

Lady-killer 女性收割机

Log-rolling 互相吹捧

Machismo 大男子主义

Macho 大男子主义的

Creeps 溜须拍马的人

Crawler 马屁精

Acquisitive 贪婪

Affect 矫揉造作

Ageism 年龄歧视

Arrogant 傲慢的

Arty 附庸风雅

Arty crafty 华而不实

Batten on sb. 损人利己

Malinger：（进行时态）装病翘课、翘班

Blowzy（女人）邋遢

Bluestocking 装有学问的女人

Boor 粗野的人

Brash：盛气凌人、自以为是；花哨俗气的打扮

Brat 顽童

Bravado 虚张声势 逞能

Brazen 厚颜无耻的

Busybody 好管闲事的人

Butch 男人婆

Bleeding heart 心慈手软的人

Chit 毛头小子 / 姑娘

Cold fish 冷漠的人

Condescend 屈尊

Connive 纵容；默许

四、比喻

比喻是重要表达方式中的一种，它不仅可以帮助我们将一些抽象概念形象表达出来，还可以提升我们的修辞水平，填补单词的空缺，实在是一举两得的方法。国内很多英语学习者知道这种表达方式，却不善于使用，希望下面例词能给大家一些启发，并在今后巧妙使用。

Bloom：freshness and perfection 完美最佳

Blossom：flourishing 崭露头角

Abrasive：hurt people's feelings；harsh and offensive 伤人的

Abyss：hole so deep that seems to have no bottom；abyss of ignorance，despair or loneliness 悲惨状况

Cobble together：put together clumsily and hastily sth. like a composition 堆砌辞藻

Concerted effort：共同努力

Crane：stretch（neck）伸脖子

Crowd：days crowded with activity 忙碌的

Crucible：severe test and trial 严酷的考验

Crumble：gradually deteriorating or come to an end 衰落

Chimney：chain smoker 烟鬼

Crystal gazing：attempt to foresee the future 有远见

Crystallize：to make clear 弄清楚

Cure sb. of sth：挽救……于……

Dawn：the dawn of hope, love, intelligence, civilization 起点

Dazzle：令人目眩

Devour：吞噬

Dose：unpleasant experience 不悦的经历

Dress sth. up：make sth. seem better by careful presentation 打磨

Dross：least valuable things or people 人渣

Electrify：stimulate sb. as if by electricity 刺激

Embroider：untrue details added for effect 粉饰太平

Engrave：（on mind/memory）镌刻

Barren：without interest result or meaning 枯燥

Bequeath：pass on（knowledge etc. to coming generations）遗赠

Fecund：fertile/fecund imagination 丰富的（想象力）

Ferment：excite, stir up 酝酿

Legacy：things passed to sb. by predecessors or from earlier events 无形遗产

Pump：like pump enough fund for sth. 提取、抽调

On fire：burning with emotion or sensation 炙热的

Fire：being criticized severely 攻击

Flimsy：weak or feeble；unconvincing 脆弱的

Flounder：struggle helpless or clumsily as in mug or deep snow；hesitate or make mistakes when talking or making a decision 不知所措

Flower of sth.：精华、鼎盛时期

Flowering：full development of an idea（literary or political movement）鼎盛

Fossil：老顽固

Fuel：things that increases anger or other strong feelings 添油加醋

Galaxy：group of brilliant talented people 群星

Gulf：difference；division（in opinion etc.）分歧

Helm of state：government 政府

Helmsman：舵手

Helpmate：可相伴之人（esp. husband and wife）

Hereabouts：在附近

Leverage：influence 影响

Hovering above/over：（of people）wait in a timid uncertain manner 依附在旁边

Hover about 犹豫徘徊

Howl：long loud wailing cry of a dog or wolf etc. 嚎叫

Wall：the divide between nations people etc. 隔离

Ceiling：top limit of salary stock price etc. 上限

Hub：central point of activity，interests or importance 轴心

Immerse oneself in：involve deeply in 沉浸

Inmost：（feelings thoughts）the most private or secrete 最私密的

Jaundiced：state of mind in which one is jealous spiteful and suspicious 妒火中烧

Ladder：series of stages of one's success 等级

Mainspring：main motive or reason for something 动因

Marrow：essential part of something 精髓

Marry：combine successfully with something else 契合

Hurdle：obstacles 障碍

Mirage：any illusion or hope that cannot be fulfilled 海市蜃楼

Mirror：a novel that mirrors modern society 反映

Take off：fast developing 腾飞

Mushroom：appear widespread 遍地开花

Hammer：heavy hit（economy）沉重打击

Morass：thing that confuses people or prevent progress 困境

Mosaic：design or pattern made up of many individual items 马赛克

Molding：developing of young people's character 塑造

Muzzle：prevent（a person，society，newspaper）from expressing ideas 压制

Myopia myopic：inability to look into the future 短视

Zenith：high 顶峰

Nadir：low 低谷

Nebulous：unclear vague 模糊

Oasis：experience，place，etc. which is pleasant in the middle of sth. unpleasant 绿洲（不好事情中的亮点）

Oblique：indirect；not going straight to the point 拐弯抹角

Deluge：great quantity of sth. that comes all at once 汹涌而至

Silver lining：hope 希望

Odyssey：long adventurous journey 冒险经历

Olive branch：things said or done to show one's wishes to make peace with somebody 示好

Omnivorous：reading all kinds of books；watch all kinds of programs 博览群书的

Outshine：talents stand out of a group 一枝独秀

Pageant of history：colorful history 绚烂的历史

Plumb：to understand thoroughly 完全理解

Hefty：substantial，extensive（from big and strong as refer to a person）肌肉发达的

Heavyweight：person of great importance or influence 重量级人物

Prince：excellent or outstanding man in a particular field 精英

Printed on memory：unforgettable 印在脑子里

Prisoner of something：completely controlled by 受困于

Propel：promote 促进

Beckon：召唤

Pry：force information out of sb.'s mouth 撬开（嘴）

Pump sth. into sth.：调取（资金等）

Punch：effective force or vigor 震动；震撼

Quench one's passion：nothing can quench her longing for returning home 压抑住

Rabid：(of feelings or opinions) violent or extreme；fanatical 狂热极端

Radiate：(of a person) give forth feelings 散发出感情

Rage：violence of the nature 大自然暴怒

Ramble：wander in one's talking or writing without keeping to the subject 随意说或写

Rash：sudden widespread of something unpleasant 泛滥

Ravening：hungrily seeking prey or food 猎食

a person seeking for property or sex 饥渴

Ray of something：slight indication of sth. good or hoped for 迹象

Realm：field of activity or interest；sphere 领域；王国

Reap：receive as one's or other's actions 收获

五、古语

古语是我们翻译中华文化传统之时不可缺少的选词，因此特将一些古英语词汇收集于此，帮助我们在翻译中国古典作品时使用。

Befall：happen or happen to sb. 发生

Beget：be the father of 为……之父

Billow：large waves 巨浪

Burgeon：grow quickly flourish 繁荣

The commons：the common people 百姓

Behold：to watch sb./sth. with absolute respect 看、尊重

Coupling：(rhetoric) sexual intercourse 性交

Cuckold：被背弃的丈夫

Embolden：(in passive) given the courage 鼓起(勇气)

Ere：before 之前

Errant：misbehaving 错误行为

Eventide：evening 晚上

Firmament：the sky 天空

For as much as：because 因为

Foundling：abandoned child 弃子

Gentlewoman：淑女

Gird：surround 围绕

Godspeed：(used when wishing sb. success on a journey etc.) 祝福

Graven：carved 镌刻

Hapless：unlucky unfortunate 不幸

Hark：listen 听取

Harlot：prostitute 妓女

Hither：to this place 到此

Hitherto：until now 至此

Lorn：lonely and sad 孤独忧伤

Morrow：the next day 第二天

Nigh：near to 在附近

Naught：nothing 一无所有

Olden：of a past age 过去

Pedagogue：teacher 教书先生

Perchance：perhaps；by chance 可能

Perforce：because it is necessary and inevitable 必须

Privy：private；secrete 私下 秘密

Beauteous：beautiful 美丽

Raiment：clothing 服装

Rapscallion：rogue 无赖

Ravish：rape a woman 强奸

Rend：tear apart forcefully 撕开

Boudoir：闺房

Yeoman：farmer who owns and works his land 小地主

Yesteryear：the recent past 最近

Travail：painful effort 艰苦努力

Behoof：benefit advantage 益处

六、肢体语言

肢体语言是世界各语言中不可或缺的组成部分。肢体语言既可在一些不方便使用语言的特定场合使用，也可以通过描述肢体语言使我们的表达更有力量和感染力。有时在书写或笔译时采用描述肢体语言的方法，可以更形象、更有画面感地表达我们的意思。例如，可以用"Have my fingers crossed to you."来替代"I wish you good luck."是不是更生动传神呢？

下面是一些肢体语言描述的例子。

Action 动作	Part of the body 身体部分	Emotion/attitude 可表达的情感或态度
Clench	Fist	Anger
Crease/furrow/knit	Brow	Concentration
		Puzzlement
Drum/tap	Fingers	Impatient
Lick	Lips	Anticipation
Purse	Lips	Disapproval dislike
Raise	Eyebrows	Inquiry surprise
Shrug	Shoulders	Doubt indifferent
Stick out	Tongue	Disrespect
Wrinkle	Nose	Dislike distaste
Bite	Lips	Nervous
Click	Fingers	Try to remember sth.
Hang	Head	Ashamed
Scratch	Head	Puzzle
Wrinkle	Forehead	Puzzle
Cross	Fingers	Good luck

七、职位、职称和部门名称

翻译时不可避免会涉及很多有关职位、职称和部门的名称，下面为大家整理了常用词汇，供大家学习使用。

部门：

Administration Department 行政部

After-sales Department 售后

Branch Office 分公司

Accounting Department 财会部

General affairs Department 综合部

Head Office 总部

Human Resources Department 人力资源部

Personnel department 人事部

Planning Department 规划部

Product Development Dept 产品开发部

R & D Dept. 研发部

Sales Promotion 销售

Secretarial Pool 秘书室

Warehouse Dept. 仓储部

行政部门：

Section 科

Division 处

Bureau 局

Department 厅

Ministry 部

职位：

总统 President

总理 Premier（共和制国家）prime minister（君主立宪制国家）chancellor（德国、奥地利）

部长 Minister，Secretary（美国）

省长、州长 governor

市长 mayor

秘书长 secretary general

（学会）会长 president（ of society ）

（大学）校长 president, principal, chancellor

中小学校长 principal（美）headmaster

公司董事长 Chairman

总裁 president

首席执行官 chief executive officer（CEO）

首席财务官 CCO

首席运营官 COO

首席信息官 CIO

助理 assistant

其他重要人物称谓：

国王陛下 King，His majesty

女王陛下 Queen，Her majesty

亲王、王子、公主 your highness

高官 your excellency

法官 your honor

牧师 reverend

八、语义的正式与非正式词

翻译有口译和笔译两种形式，口译也有正式场合与非正式场合之分。因此作为一名出色的译员，在用词上是应该有所区别的。下面收集整理出了一些常用语义的正式与非正式词对照表，供大家在不同的场合选择使用。

正式词汇 普通词汇 汉语对应词

aggregate absorb 吸收

encompass include 包含

indigenous local 当地

mortality death 死亡

grievance complaints 不满

grievous sad 忧伤

affluent rich 富裕的

pragmatic practical 实用的

preceding former/previous 前面的 以前的

precipitation haste/hurry 加速

pertain related to 与……有关

perverse unreasonable 无理

perturb disturb 打扰

abrogate cancel 取消

incipient early stage 起初

languish lack of vitality 疲软

laudable praiseworthy 值得赞扬

loath unwilling 不愿意

loquacious talkative 善谈

magisterial showing authority 权威的

magniloquent pompous 华丽讲话

magnitude large size 巨大

malady illness 疾病

malaise ailment 小恙

manifold various 各种

malediction curse 诅咒

malefactor wrongdoer 犯错的人

maleficent doing evil 恶行

manifest demonstrate 展示

ménage household 家庭

mendacious untruthful 假的

merriment gaiety/celebration 欢快

abominable disgusting/detestable 令人恐怖的

absolve clear sb of guilt 赎罪

accede to take office 入职

adjudge declare officially 宣布

adventitious accidental 偶然地

albeit although 虽然

a la mode fashionable 时尚的

amateurish unskilled 技能不强的

amplitude breadth；largeness 体量或数量巨大

attire dress 服装

expedite promote 促进

artisan skilled workman 工匠

assail attack 进攻

assent agreement/approval 同意 赞同

assiduity careful attention 凝聚注意力

assiduous attentive 注意力集中

assuage soothe 安抚

attest（to）proof 证明

slumber sleep 睡觉

augment increase 增加

avarice greed 贪婪

averse oppose to 反对

befit appropriate 恰当的

betoken indicate 表明

bewail express sorrow over 为⋯⋯忧伤

bemoan show sorrow for 哀伤 抱怨⋯⋯

beneath under 在⋯⋯之下

beset surround on all sides 被困

besmear made dirty 弄脏

bestow present sth as a gift 授予

blandishment flattering 哄骗

cease stop 停止

circumscribe confine or limit 限制

circumvent avoid 避免

civility politeness 礼貌

coeval same time 同时

cogitate ponder 思考

colloquy conversation 对话

commence begin 开始

inception origination 起初

commiserate sympathize 同情

concomitant accompanying 陪伴

concur agree 同意

concurrence agreement 一致

confound puzzle 迷惑

consign hand over 传递

consonance harmony and agreement 和谐一致

consummate to make perfect or complete 完善

cogitate thinking deeply 深思

cognizance knowledge or awareness 知识

collation snack 便餐

commodious spacious 宽敞

comport behave 行为

conformation structure 结构

convivial cheerful and sociable 快乐

convoke summon 召集

countenance support and approve 支持

craven cowardly 胆怯

cupidity greed 贪婪

preceptor teacher 老师

jubilant happiness 快乐

dire dreadful or terrible 可怕

discourse lengthy speech or writing 滔滔不绝地讲话

displacement take the place of sb. 替代

Domicile home address 住址

Dominion rule or territory 规则 领域

Elapse pass（of time）时间流逝

Elevating uplifting 向上的

Elucidate explain 解释

Emolument salary 工资

Engender cause 原因

Erudite learned scholarly 勤学

Eulogize praise 赞美

Euphony pleasant sound 悦耳的声音

Exhort urge or advise 建议

Falsehood untrue statement 谎话

Festal joyous 快乐的

Forbear refrain or self-control 自律

Forthwith immediately 立刻

Fugitive lasting for a short time 转瞬即逝的

Genesis beginning 开始

Hereafter from now on 从此以后

Hereby by this means 因此

Hereof of this 就此

Heretofore until now formerly 至此

Homage things said or done to show respect 敬仰

Hubris arrogance pride 傲慢

Immanent inherent 内在的

Immutable that cannot be changed 不变的

Impalpable that can't be touched physically 只可意会

Imperious arrogant 傲慢

Imperil endanger 危险

Impinge have an effect on 产生后果

Inasmuchas because of or to the extend that 因为

Indolent lazy inactive 懒惰

Ingress going in 进入

Inquietude anxiety 焦虑

Laud praise 赞扬

Literati educated people 文人

Littoral coast 海岸

Lubricious lewd 变态

Masticate chew 咀嚼

Embark on begin 开始

Mordant sarcastic 讽刺

Misadventure misfortune 不幸

Mores customs or conventions 习惯风俗

Notwithstanding despite of 尽管

Nucleus key point 焦点

Obdurate stubborn 顽固

Noxious harmful or poisonous 有害的

Obliterate：remove all marks of 去除

Obviate get rid of 除去

Pernicious harmful or destructive 有害的

Perpetuity permanence 永久

Perquisite money added to one's pay 外快

Perspicuous express clearly 清晰说明

Phantasm illusion 幻觉

Preciosity over refinement in language 字斟句酌

Predilection preference 喜好

Preferment promotion 促进

Prefigure foreshadow 前兆

Prescript law, rule or command 律令

Heed attention 注意力

Presentiment foreboding 隐隐感到

Prevaricate equivocate 模棱两可

Primal original 原始的

Profane secular 世俗的

Proffer offer 提供

Progeny offspring 后代

Propinquity nearness 最近的

Provenance (place of) origin 起源地

Prowess expertise 专家的

Prudence forethought wisdom 远见

Prurient excessive interest in sex 性亢奋

Purple overwritten 辞藻华丽

Purport general meaning 大意

Purvey provide or supply 提供；供应

Purview range or scope 视野

Putative generally considered; reputed 誉为

Quietude stillness calm 安静；宁静

Juxtapose put together to show difference 对比

Rapacity greed 贪婪逐利

Rectitude honesty straightforwardness 诚实；直率

Remunerate pay or reward 偿付

Delineate describe and explain 具体解释

Exiguous very small in size or amount 微小的

Bounty generosity 慷慨

Debility weakness 弱点

Lineaments features 特点

Venerate respect 尊重

九、避免重复使用

重复使用相同的单词和句型是语言表达艺术的忌讳,这也是英语大量使用代词的原因。因此,一些高频的语义我们应该储备不止一个单词或表达法去表述。下面收集了 200 多组同义或近义词来供大家积累使用。

Ardent/enthusiastic/eager/fervent/fervor/ardor

Arduous/hard/frustrating/difficult/tortuous

Promote/gear up/further/foster/boost/expedite/beef up/hasten/forward

Happen/take place/arise/occur

Ambition/desire/aspiration/pursuit

Attain/get/achieve/acquire/obtain/gain

Abate/weaken/attenuate/cut/reduce/ease/mitigate/moderate

Suite/fit/attune/applicable/conform to/comply with

accord with/conform to/comply with/keep with/keep to/in line with/be commensurate to

issue/publish/proclaim/promulgate

Propose/put forward/advance/present

Surprise/amaze/startle/astonish/astound/stun/shock/appall

Shrewd/nimble/astute/adroit

cruel/atrocity/merciless/brutal/ruthless/inhumane/ferocious

Achievement/accomplishment/attainment

Garment/dress/clothes/attire/clothing/apparel

Familiar/acquaint/au fait with

Avow/declare/admit/confess

Result/consequence/backwash/outcome

benign/kind/benevolent/forgiving

Bamboozle/puzzle/mystify/confound/confuse/bewilder flummox/disconcert/muddling

Banal/uninteresting/boring/dull/commonplace/fed up/

humdrum/monotonous/insipid

cachet/reputation/fame

Cajole/coax/inveigle

Disaster/catastrophe/calamity/havoc

Cause/give rise to/lead to/bring about/arouse/set/touch off/trigger/initiate/evoke/engender/instigate

honest/straightforward/candid/frank/candor

Standard/general rule/principle/canon/norm

Caprice/capricious/changeable

Charm/enchant/captivate/enthrall

Charming/captivating/fascinating/enchanting

Captious/carp/picky/cavil/choosy/fastidious

Accommodate/entertain/receive/cater to/attend to

Celebrated/famous/well-known/noted/renown/prominent/character/eminent/illustrious

chafe/impatient/unrest

Chagrin/disappointment/annoyance/depression

Committee/commission/board/council

Uncertain/chancy/risky

Chink/seam/cleavage/crack/crevice

Push/urge/chivvy/expedite/impel/prompt

Circumscribe/confine/limit/restrict

Wary/cautious/circumspect

Circumvent/avoid/eschew/keep away from

coddle/care/attend to/tend

caress/fondle

Cogent/convincing/logic

Conceal/hide/cover

Conduce/conducive to/benefit

Handle/deal with/cope with/manage/conduct/process

Implement/execute/carry out/practice/put into effect

Agreement/concurrence/consensus/approval/assent

Consonant/in agreement/suitable/consistent

Constancy/faithfulness/loyalty

part/component/constituent

Confine/constrain/bind

Construe/interpret/explain

Important/significant/vital/weighty/major/essential/substantial/of primary consideration/paramount/capital/gravity/pivotal/momentous

Urgent/imperative/pressing/critica/mandatory

commiserate with/sympathy/compassion/mercy/humane

Commodious/spacious/roomy

in conjunction with/together with

contour/outline

Improvement/betterment

in agreement/appropriate/concordant with

agreement/concurrence

Break/breach/contravene/infringe

Contrive/invent/design

Convene/summon/convoke

Plentiful/abundant/copious/bountiful/profuse/prodigious

Coruscate/sparkle/flash

Pamper/spoil/cosset/dote on

apogee/zenith/climax/crowning

Countenance/facial expression

Countenance/support/approve

vulgar/countrified/rustic

crave for/eager/desire/yearn for/hanker after

Crucial/critical/fatal/decisive

Crystallize/clarify/elucidate/throw light on/illuminate

culminate in/result in/lead to

Culmination/conclusion/result/consequence

Control/restrain/curb/harness

Reduce/curtail/cut/decrease/lessen/cut down/diminish

norm/rule/precept/guide

Dearth/shortage/scarcity/scant/deficiency/lack/want/devoid

Prescribe/stipulate/institute

Contiguous/neighboring/vicinity/adjoining/propinquity/proximity

diametrically/completely/entirely

maxim/dictum/motto/proverb/adage/fable/catchphrase/precept

Aspect/dimension/side

Dire/dreadful/terrible/formidable/horrifying/frightening

Discourage/depress/dispirit/dismay/distress

Contort/distort/deform

Docile/tame/obedient

Sorrowful/dolorous/sad/grievous

dilemma/double bind

Dour/stern/severe/gloomy-looking/joyless/downcast

Dread/fear/fright/horror/terror

Dreary/depressed/dismal/gloomy/droop/droopy/broody moody

Dribble/drip

echelon/hierarchy/rank

elegy/lament

eligible/suitable/fit/qualified/entitled

emblem/symbol/icon

chairman/anchorman/processor/announcer/host/emcee/compere

endow/endue/grant/bless

audacious/fearless/daring/adventurous

augment/increase/expand/raise/add/mount

dislike/aversion/antipathy

brazen/shameless/insolent

entice/induce/lure/tempt

equable/moderate

erratic/irregular/uneven

exigency/urgency/emergency

expatiate/elaborate/expound

extempore/impromptus/improvise

praise/extol/compliment/sing/eulogize

exhilarate/joyous/jubilant/ecstasy/exuberant/cheerful/merry/
happy/exult/rejoice/pleasure/glad/pleased/festive/festal/gaiety/
jolly/mirth/rapture

Wonderful/excellent/fabulous/exceptional/eventful/
marvelous/superb/splendid/magnificent/brilliant

Ability/capability/capacity/faculty

Factitious/unnatural/pretentious/histrionic

Failing/flaw/defect/shortcoming/weakness/
fault/foible/peccadillo

fall/guy/scapegoat

far-flung/extensive/expanded

tiredness/fatigue/exhausted/toilworn/run down/laborious

faze/nervous/flurry/fluster

fecund/fertile/productive

feeble/weak/faint/frail

felicitate/congratulate

failure/fiasco

fidelity/faithfulness/loyalty/allegiance

severe/grave/gross/serious/gravity

genius/gifted/talent/flair

widespread/flourish/thriving/prosper

flout/despise/scorn/contempt

foil/hinder/prevent from/obstruct/impede/handicap/
hamper/inhibit/prelude

rash/bold/foolhardy/reckless

above/aforementioned/foregoing/preceding

lonely/uncared/forlorn

straightforward/frankness/forthright

deceitful/foxy/cunning/sneaky/tricky/crafty/fraudulent/

dishonest/guile

fractional/fragmentary/segmental/bits and pieces

fringe/edge/rim/brink

foam/froth

thrifty/frugal

dumb/dumbbell/dullard/dupe/dummy/dunderhead/dotty/

donkey/daft/ass/blockhead/bonehead/booby/bovine/fatuous/

feather-brained/folly/fucker/idiot/goof/hare-brained/stupidity/

idiocy/jackass/moron/ninny/nitwit/numskull/oafish

brave/valor/gallant/courageous

garish/gaudy/unpleasantly/bright/over-colored

gravity/solemnity

habituate oneself to/accustom sb. to/be used to

haphazard/disorder/random/disorganized

harass/harry/（with repeated questions or request）

arrogant/haughty/proud and disdainful/high and mighty

reprimand/scold/blame/curse/bawl out/rebuke/fulminate

celebrity/guru/master/heavyweight

busy/hectic/bustling

pay attention to/heed

scare/frighten/hector

amusing/funny/hilarious

everywhere/breadth and length/uphill and down dale

hick/bumpkin/redneck/hill-billy

nonsense/hogwash/bullshit

homely/plain/simple

huckster/hawker/street vendor

huddle/crowd/heap

hue/color

humility/modesty/a humble attitude

hurdle/difficulty/obstacle

hurl/fling/throw

husky/hoarse

ignoble/shameful

titanic/mighty/massive/tremendous/immense

weaken/damage/impair

imminent/impending/forthcoming

implore/beg/beseech

inborn/inbred/instinct/innate

incessant/continual/nonstop

inimical/unfriendly/hostile

injurious/harmful/hazardous

inherent/innate/inborn/instinctive

disobedient/rebellious/insubordinate

tempting/attractive/inviting

jeer/mock

joke/jest/kidding

laconic/concise

greed/voracious/ravenous/hunger for/insatiable

praise/laud/glorify/compliment/eulogize

in lieu of/instead of/in × × 's place

irritable/liverish/peevish

eccentric/oddball/loony/lunatic/freak/insane

upheaval/riot/chaos/mayhem/havoc

interfere/meddle

ponder/meditation/muse on/deliberation/contemplate

mollify/lessen/soothe

cloudy/gloomy/murky/hazy

vague/unclear/nebulous/opaque

hateful/disgusting/odious/odium

sign/omen

parity/egalitarianism/equality

worsen/exacerbate/aggravate

outline/framework/precise

predicament/difficulty/dilemma/between hell and high
water/embarrassment/frustration

progressive/gradual

enforce sth./impose sth on sb./foist sth. on sb.

mob/rabble

appear/emerge/crop up/turn up/arise

ambiguous/equivocal（equivocate equivocation）

attentive/focused/spellbound/rapt/indulged

repeal/revoke/nullify

model/exemplar

support/endorsement

十、近义词间的准确理解和使用

精准表达是判定翻译是否成功的重要标准之一,因此对于近义词间的准确理解和使用便是译者该具备的能力之一。

下面整理了一些近义词的细微差别,供大家参考,以便日后实践应用。

（1）act action deed feat exploit 行为

act and action 有时是一样的

deed 更加正式

exploits and feat 优良品质,指经过长时间培养的优点

（2）arrange，organize and plan 组织计划

几个词都有安排和准备的意思

在"安排"的语义中

arrange 把事务按照正确合理的方式安排

organize 进入系统工作状态

plan 以图表的方式安排地点、项目等

在"准备"的语义中

We arrange a meeting. 指"邀请"所有合适人员

We organize a meeting. 指"做出必要的准备",如准备会议室、设备、饮品等

You plan a meeting. 侧重"细节",如会议时长,议程等

（3）agree approve consent and acquiesce 同意

agree：表示你会按别人的意见做或你同意某个行为

approve：正式同意一个计划、建议或请求

consent：（正式）同意某件事或给予许可

acquiesce：默许

（4）become get go turn 变

become 和 turn 比 get 和 go 更加正式

become or get 形容暂时的身心变化和永久的自然变化，可与 angry famous fat ill old 等搭配使用

我们用 go，例如 go bald/deaf/insane 等形容某种衰退的身心状况

go and turn 可用于表示颜色的变化

（5）carry bear cart hump 搬运

carry 是泛指词

用 bear 表"移动状态"时，比较正式

cart 是比喻的说法，意为像车一样搬运

hump 是指负重很大，难以移动

（6）jump hop leap cavort 跳

jump：泛指词

hop：（形容人）单脚跳

（形容动物）跳等

leap：远距离跳，飞跃

cavort：激动地跳跃

（7）change alter modify vary revise 改变

change 是泛指词

alter：外观、特点和用途的改变

modify：（正式）结构上的部分改变，也可以是态度和意见的软化

vary：暂时和重复的变化

revise：修复、提升

（8）laugh smile grin giggle chortle chuckle smirk 笑

laugh：泛指词

smile：泛指词

grin：露齿地笑

giggle：小声或傻气地笑

chortle：大声笑

chuckle：咯咯地笑

smirk：自我满足地笑

（9）close and shut 关闭

close 比 shut 更正式

（10）coast shore beach seaside 海边

coast: wide range

shore: narrow stripe of land along the water

beach: sloppy part of the shore

seaside：前往度假的 coast

（11）comprise be composed of constitute consist of 构成

comprise 等同于 be composed of 和 consist of

Compose or constitute 组成 / 构成了

（12）conserve preserve reserve 保护；保留

conserve：防止被改变或破坏或丢失

preserve：保持不变和良好的状态

reserve：保留给自己；矜持；内敛

（13）continual continuous

continual：间断性连续

continuous：一直延续

（14）country state nation and land 国家

country 是个中性词，指地理意义上的国家

state 强调国家的政治体制

nation：政治性，而且比较正式，有时可以指国民

land：充满感情、诗意地用词

（15）cry sob weep wail whimper 哭泣

cry：最频繁的用词

weep：表达情感，流泪

sob：啜泣

wail：哀嚎

whimper：孩子抱怨的哭泣

（16）dealers，traders，merchants and vendor 商人商贩

dealer：销售单一商品，而且具有专业知识的商人、经纪人

trader：市场中正式售卖的商人

merchant：批量销售特定商品的商人

vendor：街头售卖小商品的商贩

（17）order command decree dictate ordain prescribe 命令

order：泛指词

command：给人或动物下的命令

decree：统治者独自发出的指令

dictate：强加于人下命令

ordain：（正式）可用来表示上帝的旨意

prescribe：提出法律规定

（18）different from/than 区别不同

different from：是英式英语的表达法，而美式英语既可用 different

from 也可用 different than

（19）wide broad 宽大

wide：泛指词

broad：可以用来形容体型，或更加文雅，也可用于形容风景

（20）drip leak ooze run seep 滴漏

drip：有规律滴落

leak：漏出

ooze：因很稠而缓慢流出

run：连续不断流出

seep：从细孔中缓慢流出

以上除 seep 外都可指容器或活门使液体流出的方式

（21）demonstration display exhibition show fair 展示

demonstration and display：不必有特定永久地点

display：常常用于公共娱乐方面

exhibition/show/fair：通常在大厅或中心举行

show：可用于指动物或植物展示

exhibition：画作等

fair：各种娱乐的展演

（22）factory mill plant works 工厂

factory：用于形容制造产品的场地建筑

works：大型综合性的建筑和机器，一般不生产完成品

plant：产业加工类的，如 power chemical

mill：指加工原材料的工厂（cotton woolen steel paper）

（23）fairly pretty quite rather 程度副词的区别

fairly：最弱

pretty：更强一点

quite：更强一些

rather：最强语气

pretty and rather：用于积极的语气，听起来更有热情

rather：可用于比较级 rather bigger

quite and rather 可用在不定冠词前 rather/quite a nice day

（24）male female man woman masculine feminine 男女性别

male female：指两性的生理特点，如 Male voice，female figure

man woman：谈到职业时 woman doctor 不用 female doctor，但是 male doctor 而不是 man doctor。

masculine and feminine：描述行为、相貌，如 She has a masculine voice 而不是 a male voice

（25）heredity heritage legacy relics 遗产

heredity：从父母传下来的形貌特点

heritage：祖先留下艺术、文化成就

legacy：遗嘱中留下的钱财，也可指先人留下的精神财富

（26）fog mist haze smog 雾

fog：最浓密而 haze 最淡薄

mist：常在早上出现的薄雾

haze：可能在很热的天气出现

smog：是烟和雾的混合体

（27）complain grumble gripe grizzle grouch grouse 抱怨

complain：泛指词

grumble：坏脾气的抱怨

gripe：习惯性地抱怨

grizzle：（尤指小孩子）哭哭啼啼抱怨

grouch：贬义词

grouse：贬义词

（28）train groom cultivate 培养

train：泛指词

groom：培养年轻人一个特殊的职业

cultivate：培养道德和好习惯等

（29）groan growl moan grunt guttural adj. 嚎叫

growl：发出低沉威胁的声音（动物）

groan：表达疼痛、忧伤或绝望的声音

grunt：嗓子眼发出的沙哑声音

guttural：似乎是从喉咙发出的声音

（30）happen occur take place 发生

happen and occur：指意外而不是计划的事件，occur 更加正式

happen：也指结果，如 what happened after you told her that?

take place：指计划好的事件

（31）healthy fit and well 健康

healthy：指身体健康良好的特征

fit：指良好的健康状况，特别是指经过锻炼的结果

well：指特定情境的健康状况

（32）height tall high altitude 高度

height：指人或物的纵向高度，也可指物体与地面或海平面的距离

tall：指人、植物、建筑

high：不用于指人

altitude：海拔的高度

（33）hit strike and beat 击打

hit 比 beat or strike 用得频繁

strike：更加正式

beat：通常不是意外且可是重复性的

（34）hope and wish 希望

hope：指与过去、现在和将来相关的愿望

wish：表达对过去、现在和将来的遗憾，如 I wish I haven't gone to the party. I wish I could speak English but I can't.

用于不定式，语义相近

（35）invaluable valueless priceless numberless innumerable 都与"价值"有关

invaluable 无价、贵重

valueless 指毫无价值

priceless 无法以价格论其价值

Innumerable and numberless 都指巨大的数字

（36）journey voyage travels trip tour and excursion 旅行

journey：经常性地长短旅行

voyage：海洋或空间的长途旅行

travels：以游玩为目的的旅行

tour：更注重娱乐性

trip：短途的旅行，并返回原地

excursion：一群人的旅游

（37）look gaze stare gawp peer 看

gaze：长时间凝视一个方向（有时可能不一定专注）

stare：长期关注的凝望

peer：由于有难度而很认真地看

gawp：张嘴傻乎乎地看

（38）machine tool appliance apparatus instrument implement device gadget 机器工具

machine：电驱动的包含转动部件的机器

appliance：家用的

tool：手拿的

instrument：用于技术目的的

implement：用于户外，特别是园艺或农活用

device：赞赏口吻说出的工具

gadgets：可能是贬义的

（39）mistake error blunder fault defect 缺点错误

mistake：泛指词

error：正式

blunder：由于马虎或判断错误带来的错误

fault：强调个人的责任，也可以表示一个人或物的缺点

defect：更加严重

（40）occurrence event and incident 事件

occurrence：中性词，不特指某一个事件

event：重要的事件

incident：不重要的偶发事件

（41）old aged elderly ancient and antique 古老

old：应用广泛，还可表示旧的

aged：正式，可指非常老，而且体能差

elderly：对老年人的敬语

ancient and antique：指实物

antique：古董

（42）forward forwards 向前

forward：用于形容词和副词

forwards：只用于副词

（43）rare scarce 稀少

rare：很少见的，可能曾经很普遍，如 The panda is now a rare animal.

scarce：由于缺乏而很难得到

（44）cause reason justification ground motive 原因

cause：引发事件的原因

reason：高频词，解释行为的原因

reason cause and justification：都可表示某个可以接受的解释或该解释是合理的，如：The police had no reason to suspect him/no justification for suspecting him/no cause for suspicion.

ground：正式特指行为的法律依据，多用复数

motive：人们内心去做某事的动因，如 He claimed that his motive for stealing was hunger.

（45）recently not long ago lately 最近

recently：广泛用于肯定、否定和疑问句式中

not long ago：只用于肯定

lately：用于否定和疑问式，在肯定式中与 only，not much 或

a lot 连用。

（46）relation relationship relations 关系

relationship：高频词，可表达强烈的情感联系

relation relationship：均可表示家庭关系

relations and relationship：可表示与人际关系无关的关系

（47）above over 上方

above and over：都可用于比较级

over：可以是覆盖的意思，可用于数量，货币和时间

above：指固定的点，如 2000 meters above sea level

（48）present and current 目前

都可指正在发生或目前的情况

current：可以表示暂时的

（49）advertisement, commercial, promotion and trailer 广告

advertisement：泛指词

commercial：电视收音机广告

promotion：促销

trailer：电视 / 电影预告片

（50）acknowledge concede, admit confess grant 承认

acknowledge：（正式）接受某事是真的或已经发生

concede：（正式）不情愿地承认某事在逻辑上是真实的

admit：不情愿地承认

confess：承认一件耻辱或尴尬的事情

grant：承认一件事是正确的，而不对其给予更高的评价

例：She's an intelligent woman, I grant you, but she is no genius.

Granted he is a beginner, but he should know the basic rules.

（51）approximately, give or take, more or less, or so, thereabouts, round about roughly, somewhere around, about 都有"大概"之意（本组以例句形式区分）

approximately：The flight takes approximately three hours.

give or take：The repairs will cost $200, give or take.

more or less：How much will its cost, more or less.

or so：We are expecting thirty or so people to come.

thereabouts：She must be 25 or thereabouts.

roughly：Profits have fallen by roughly 15%.

round about：You can expect to earn round about 40,000 a year.

around：The price is somewhere around $800.

about：The ticket costs about $20.

（52）ashamed embarrassed 害羞

ashamed：因有意做了错事而感到羞耻

embarrassed：因犯了错误或在人前出丑而感觉尴尬

（53）ask demand enquire query 询问

ask：泛指词

demand：强烈的请求

enquire/inquire：（正式）寻求信息

demand：严肃地问

query：（正式）提问

（54）fall asleep，go to sleep，get to sleep，drift off，nod off，drop off 睡觉

fall asleep：睡着,可表不知不觉或在不合适的场合睡了

go to sleep：准备睡觉

get to sleep：特别是之前长时间睡不着或难以入睡

drift off：慢慢睡着了

nod off：（口语）短睡,尤指是坐着睡

drop off：浅睡

（55）avenge revenge vengeance 报复

avenge 是动词 revenge 是名词

avenge oneself on sb. 向某人复仇

例：She vowed to avenge her brother's death.

He later avenged himself on his wife's killer.

take revenge on sb.：正式语言中,revenge 也可用作动词

vengeance：和 revenge 相同,但更加正式

（56）big，large，great 大

big：通常搭配：man house car boy dog smile problem surprise question difference

large：通常搭配 numbers part area room company eyes

family volume population problem

great：通常搭配 success majority interest importance difficulty problem pleasure beauty artist surprise

（57）boring tedious uninteresting dull dry 枯燥

boring：无趣，让人感觉很累或不耐烦

tedious：无聊而且持续时间很长

uninteresting：无法吸引注意力和兴趣

dull：无聊，没有刺激，如 Life in a small town could be dull.

dry：缺少人情味而显得枯燥

（58）break, rest, breather, breathing space, respite, time-out, recess 休息

break：短期停止正在做的事情

rest：一段放松、睡觉的时间

breather：（口语）活动中间的小段休息，主动权在自己

breathing space：要争取的休息时间

respite：困难和讨厌的事情中间的休息

time out：工作与学习中间的休息

recess：在美式英语中表示休息

（59）british briton brits 英国人

british：泛指词

briton：报纸用语，如 The survivor of the avalanche included 12 Britons.

brits：非正式，而且有些贬义

（60）burn blacken scald scorch singe 燃烧烤制

burn：用火破坏，伤害或杀害；被烟火熏黑

blacken：（常用作被动）熏黑

scald：热的液体或蒸汽烫伤

scorch：高温轻微损伤表面

singe：因失误烫伤表面

（61）call, cry out, exclaim, blurt, burst out 呼喊

call：大声叫或说话吸引注意力

cry out：处于危险中呼喊帮助

exclaim：由于激动而大声喊

blurt：脱口而出

burst out：由于情绪激动而突然短促喊出

（62）care caution prudence discretion wariness 小心

care：认真注意做事以避免犯错

caution：谨慎以免出错

prudence：（正式）做决定或判断时认真仔细

discretion：（正式）小心说话做事以保守秘密或避免给他人带来尴尬和困难

wariness：（正式）因害怕有危险或出问题而与人打交道时小心

（63）certain bound definite sure assured 确定

certain：相信某事可靠或真实

bound：确定会发生

Sure：可以确定会发生，因此相信

Definite（口语）确定会发生，不会改变

（64）cheat, deceive, betray, take sb in, trick, fool 欺骗

cheat：为了利益让人相信某个不真实的事

deceive：欺骗相信你的人，最强贬义

betray：因为某种原因背叛

take sb. in：（常用作被动）欺骗

trick：巧妙骗过，可有赞许之意

fool：愚弄

（65）burst crack crumble fracture shatter smash snap split 断裂

Burst：胀破

例：The balloon hit a tree and burst.

crack：开裂

例：The ice started to crack.

crumble：弄成碎屑

例：Crumble the cheese into a bowl.

fracture：折断

例：He fell and fractured his hip.

shatter：裂成碎片

例：The vase hit the floor and shattered.

smash：粉碎

例：Vandals had smashed two windows.

snap：啪的一声断裂，亦指"打响指"

split：裂开

例：The bag split open on the way.

（66）clean wash rinse cleanse 洗涤

clean：用水或化合物去除脏东西或尘土

wash：用水和洗涤用品去除污物

rinse：只用清水漂洗

cleanse：清理皮肤或伤口

（67）obvious apparent evident plain crystal clear 明确

obvious：容易看清和理解

apparent：（正式，不作定语）容易看清和理解

evident：（非常正式）有据可循

plain：由于简单而容易看清和理解

crystal clear：如水晶般清透明确

clear：毫不怀疑

（68）collect，gather，accumulate，run things up，amass 收集集中

collect：从不同的人和地方收集物品或信息

gather：把曾经散开的东西再收集起来；从不同来源收集信息

accumulate：（正式）通过一段时间逐渐积累

run sth. up：（口语）让账单、欠账等积少成多

amass：（非常正式）大量积累金钱、债务、信息等

（69）comment note remark observe 评论

comment：表达意见或提供事实

note：（非常正式）因重要或有趣提到某事

remark：通过口头或书写表达你注意到的情况

observe：（正式）通过口头或书写表达你注意到的情况

（70）complain protest object grumble moan whine 抱怨

complain：表达你对人或事得不满意

protest：公开声明你的不同意见或反对意见

object：声明你的不同意或反对意见，并给出理由

grumble：（口语）脾气很坏地抱怨

moan：让人闹心地抱怨

whine：哭诉你的不满

（71）condition state 条件状况

condition：常搭配 good excellent physical poor human perfect no better

state：常搭配 present current mental solid no emotional physical natural

（72）spending expenditure expenses outlay outgoings 花销

spending：支出的资金

expenditure：（正式）政府、机构或个人的支出

expenses：必需的花销

outlay：用于做生意和项目的资金

（73）crash slam collide smash 撞击

crash：（口语）撞击物体或另一机动车且造成损坏

slam into：用力撞击

collide：（正式）两辆车迎头撞击

smash：（口语）用力撞击

（74）damage hurt harm impair prejudice 伤害

damage：造成破坏

hurt：对他人的寿命、健康和幸福带来伤害

harm：对他人的寿命、健康和幸福带来伤害（比 hurt 强度更大）。

impair：（非常正式）损害了他人的能力、健康和机会

（75）declare state indicate announce 宣布说明

declare：（非常正式）正式公开宣布

state：（非常正式）以仔细和清晰的方式说或写出

indicate：（非常正式）阐述某事，有时不直接

announce：官宣某项决定或计划

（76）hard demanding difficult taxing testing challenging 艰难

hard and difficult：几乎相同，hard to 搭配 believe/say/find/take

challenging：有困难但同时有趣

demanding：需要很大努力、技能和耐心才能解决的困难

taxing：（常用于否定）难做，需要很多身心付出。例：This

shouldn't be too taxing for you.

testing：需要特殊力量和能力才能完成

（77）dusty dirty filthy soiled grubby 脏

dirty：布满灰尘、土、泥、油

dusty：布满灰尘

filthy：令人生厌的脏

soiled：（非常正式）脏东西或身体排放物

grubby：（口语）没有清洗而显得很脏

（78）disease illness disorder infection ailment bug 疾病

disease：经常由感染引起的人、动物或植物的病

illness：病或一段时间的难受，可能是精神上的

disorder：（正式）让身体部分机能失效的病

infection：由细菌病毒引起的感染

ailment：小恙

bug：（口语）轻微的传染病

（79）Revolting disgusting repulsive offensive gross nauseating foul 令人讨厌和反感

disgusting：令人非常不悦 恶心

revolting：令人非常不悦（不如 disgusting 高频）

foul：脏、味道和气味很坏

gross：（口语）（气味、味道或习惯）令人非常不悦；恶心

nauseating：让人有呕吐感

（80）double dual 双

double：常搭配 bed doors figures standards thickness

dual：常搭配 purpose function role approach citizenship

（81）effect result consequence outcome repercussion 影响

effect：因影响而改变

result：因影响而产生了某种结果

consequence：（正式）通常是负面的结果

outcome：一个过程的结果

repercussion：间接影响

（82）environment setting surroundings background backdrop 环境

environment：能够影响到人的行为和发展的状况

setting：某事发生或存在的背景

surroundings：周边的环境

backdrop：（正式）对主体有烘托作用的背景

（83）excellent outstanding perfect superb marvelous exceptional 杰出

excellent：特别好，尤其有关服务标准

outstanding：表述一个人的做事能力

perfect：完美适合

superb：（口语）令人印象深刻

marvelous：（口语）奇妙；神了

exceptional：关于人的表现或能力

（84）excited ecstatic elated rapturous euphoric exhilarated，on top of the world 高兴激动

excited：感觉高兴和热情

ecstatic：非常高兴

elated：由于有好事发生或即将发生而高兴

euphoric：短暂的开心

rapturous：狂喜

exhilarated：运动后的喜悦

on top of the world：（口语）激动和自豪

（85）expensive costly overpriced dear 昂贵

expensive：昂贵

costly：（正式）超出你能力的贵

overpriced：不值得的贵

dear：贵，仅用于表语

（86）fast quick rapid swift speedy 快速

fast：常搭配 car train bowler pace lane

quick：常搭配 glance look reply decision way

rapid：常搭配 change growth increase decline progress

swift and speedy：正式用词

（87）overweight，large or heavy，plump chubby stocky stout flabby obese 肥胖

overweight：中性词

large or heavy：比 fat 更易被接受

plump：丰满

chubby：婴儿肥

tubby：（口语）语气友好去描述矮而胖的人

stocky：矮并且粗壮

stout：老年人

flabby：松弛的肉（伤人的用词）

obese：医生用语

（88）fight clash brawl struggle scuffle tussle 打斗

fight：泛指词

clash：新闻用词

brawl：大声暴力打斗

struggle：当打斗人之一试图逃跑时

scuffle：短暂,不太暴力的打斗

tussle：短暂的打斗或口角

（89）hair style 发型

crew cut：平头

flat top：平头

crop hair：短发

bob：女士波波头

permed hair：烫发

french plait：法式辫子

pig tails：两根辫子

braid：一根辫子

bunches：两束发

bun：圆发髻；盘头

（90）merit value worth virtue 优点价值

merit：指人的价值,优点

value：价值的意义（含有 excellent 的意味）

virtue：美德

wort：使用价值

（91）bitter pungent sour acrid acid sharp 各种不好的味道

bitter：（taste and smell）苦

pungent：（smell and taste）呛人

acrid：（smell）呛人

sour：（taste）未成熟的水果酸

acid：（smell and taste）刺激的

sharp：（taste and smell）辛辣；略苦的

（92）building property premises complex structure block edifice

建筑

building：建筑物；房屋楼房

property：房屋及院落，庄园；房产

premises：企业的房屋及所属场所

complex：类型相似的建筑群

structure：指结构体建筑物

edifice：宏伟的建筑

block：公寓；办公；学校；医院等特殊用途的大楼

（93）cheerful bright cheery jolly merry，in a good mood 高兴

cheerful：高兴；快乐

bright：神色快活而且生机勃勃

cheery：（举止）欢快起劲儿

jolly：兴高采烈（口语）

merry：文绉绉地表达

in a good mood：因为高兴而友善

（94）choice favorite preference selection pick 选择；喜欢

choice：选中的人或物

favorite：同类人或物中最喜欢的

preference：偏爱（与 favorite 相比，主动意味差）

selection：从大群中选出的一组人或物

pick：（口语）选中人或物

（95）choose，pick，select，go for，single out，opt 选择

choose：选取

select：（经常被动）认真地从一组中挑选

pick：（口语）挑选

opt：选择是否采取某种行动

go for：物的选择

single out：强调单独选出

（96）clothes clothing dress garment wear gear apparel 各种服装

clothes：衣服（上下身的）

clothing：指某种类型的

例：warm clothing 暖和的衣服

dress：着装

例：为某个场合或某种样式 casual dress

garment：（正式）一件衣服

wear：尤指商店售卖的衣服

gear：特殊用途或时尚的服装

apparel：商店出售的和正式场合穿的

（97）color shade tone hue tint tinge 颜色

shade：色彩的浓淡深浅，色度

例：Sky blue is a shade of blue.

tone：色调；明暗

例：A carpet in warm tones of brown and orange.

hue：色度；色调

例：His face took on an unhealthy, whitish hue.

tint：单色调

例：Leaves with red and gold autumn tint.

tinge：少许颜色

例：There was a pink tinge to the sky. 一抹淡粉色

（98）country countryside terrain landscape scenery land 与乡村有关

country：有自然特色的乡村

landscape：（大范围的）乡村的风景和景色

countryside：乡村（强调美丽与宁静时常用）

terrain：描述农村的地形地势

land：指与城镇相对的农村的生活方式

scenery：自然的风景、景色、风光

（99）course program 与课程有关

course：系列课程，或大学的一个阶段 a two year course（英式）

一个独立单位的课程 physics course（美式）

program：大学的一个阶段 a two year program（美）

（100）discussion conversation dialogue talk consultation chat gossip 谈话

discussion：就重要问题所进行的详尽讨论

conversation：人与人或一组人之间的私人、非正式的谈话。

dialogue：书中、电影中的对话；两组人之间为解决分歧而进行的交流。

talk：就某个事情和有关人员进行的重要交流

consultation：在做决定前，两组人之间的正式讨论

chat：非正式的谈话

gossip：私下里谈论别人，八卦

（101）electric electrical 电的

electric：常搭配 light guitar drill chair shock

electrical：常搭配 equipment wiring signal engineer shock

electrical：惯与更复杂和高端的对象搭配

（102）essential vital 重要

essential：说明事实，表明权威意见

vital：为某事感到忧虑或需要使人信服

（103）examine study 考察研究

examine：为理解和让别人理解

study：让自己理解

（104）手部动作

touch：接触

feel：摸

finger：用手指触摸

handle：拿

rub：揉；搓

stroke：轻抚

pat：轻拍

tap：轻敲

squeeze：捏；挤

grab：抓；抢

snatch：一下夺走

clasp：握紧；抱紧

clutch：抱紧；抓紧

grasp：抓住

grip：紧抓；紧握

（105）identify, recognize, make out, discern, pick out, distinguish 区别

identify：确认，鉴定

recognize：辨别，认出

make out：看清，听清，分清，辨认

discern：察觉，依稀看出

pick out：从一群中认出

distinguish：（通常否定句）分辨

（106）label tag 标签

label：缝在衣物上

tag：挂在衣物上

（107）like, love, be fond of, be keen on, adore 喜欢

like：喜欢

love：非常喜欢

be fond of：喜欢了很长时间

be keen on：（常用于否定）喜欢

adore：宠爱

（108）limit limitation restriction restraint control constraint 限制

limit：指极限，限量，限额

limitation：较常用，可是人为，也可是客观地限制规则、事实和条件

restriction：（很正式）限制规定，限制法规，多为掌权者所制定的

restraint：（很正式）管制措施，制约因素可能是他人或自己制定的

control：（经常构成组合词）限制，约束和管理的行为

constraint：（很正式）限制，限定，约束，也可能是某人决定的限制

（109）loudly loud aloud 大声

loudly：形容词 loud 的副词

loud：总是用在 phrase 中：as loud as，loud enough

aloud：（正式）强调发出声音

（110）fate destiny or providence 命运

fate：可以是意外的恩赐；同时也可是残酷的，使人无能为力

destiny：更给人力量感，具有强烈使命感

providence：通常是正面的，即便降临苦难也是上帝安排的一部分

（111）mix mingle blend 混合

mix 通用泛词

mingle：可以形容声音颜色等

blend：更彻底地混合，可指烹饪、艺术、音乐、时尚

（112）reason grounds excuse motive need justification cause pretext 理由

reason：某事发生或做某事的原因、理由

grounds：说、做、相信某事的充分原因、根据、法律依据

excuse：辩解的借口和理由

motive：对一个人行为动机的解释

need：侧重需求

justification：指事物存在或做某事的正当理由

cause：（正式）某种感情或行为产生的原因、动机、缘故

pretext：（非常正式）为掩盖真正理由所找到的借口

（113）advise recommend 建议

advise：通常是告诫，用于上级对下级，否则有冒犯的含义

recommend：通常是正面的建议

（114）satisfaction fulfillment contentment glee 满足

satisfaction：由于成就而感到高兴

fulfillment：做了有益的事情或对生活的满足感

contentment：（正式）满足感

glee：有时有幸灾乐祸的意味

（115）satisfying fulfilling rewarding 令人满足的

satisfying：常用泛词，关于个人经历

fulfilling：长期的，比如你的职业带来的，与个人经历有关

rewarding：得到回报

（116）sensible sensitive 能感觉到

sensible：判断力

sensitive：情感、反应力和洞察力

（117）shine gleam glow sparkle glisten shimmer glitter twinkle 闪光

shine：强烈闪光

gleam：朦胧光

glow：稳定而微弱的

sparkle：闪耀 闪烁

glisten：光泽

shimmer：微弱的闪光

glitter：闪亮

twinkle：一明一暗的闪光

（118）走路方式

creep：蹑手蹑脚地走

limp：一瘸一拐地走

pace：徘徊

pad：放轻脚步走

plod：沉重缓慢；步履艰难地走

shuffle：拖脚走

stagger：摇摇晃晃地走

stomp：声音很大的走

stroll：漫步；闲逛

tiptoe：踮脚走

trudge：步履艰难地走

（119）witness viewer audience observer spectator onlooker passer-by bystander 观者

witness：目击者

audience：聚集在一起观看

viewer：看电视的人

observer：目击者（不是法律词语）

spectator：观看的人（尤其体育比赛）

onlooker：看见而没涉及的人

passer-by：碰巧路过而看到的人

bystander：在附近看见的人

（120）employment career profession occupation trade work 工作

employment：（正式）工作；就业

career：职业生涯

profession：需要专门技能的职业

occupation：（正式）工作或职业

trade：行业

（121）wrong wrongly wrongfully 错

wrong：用于非正式语言，置于动词后或动词宾语后

wrongly：用于分词前 wrongly spelt 和从句前 例：She guessed wrongly that he was a teacher.

wrongfully：法律用语

（122）things stuff possessions junks belongings goods valuables 物品东西

这些词均指东西、物品，尤指个人拥有或随身携带的。

thing：（口语化）个人所有或特定用途的

stuff：（口语化）指名称不详，或名称无关紧要的

possessions：个人财产或私人物品（尤指动产）

junk：无用的东西

belongings：随身物品

goods：私人财产

valuables：贵重物品

（123）描述事物的其他单词

aspects：方面

attribute：属性；特性；特质

characteristic：特点

detail：细节；详情

feature：特点

issue：议题；课题；问题

matter：事情；情况；问题

point：观点；论点；见解

subject：主题；题目学科

topic：论题；话题；题目

trait：特征；特点；特征；品质

（124）right correct exact precise accurate spot on 正确

right：that is true and cannot be doubted as a fact 正确真实的

correct：比 right 更加正式

spot on：对极了（英式）

exact precise accurate：差别不大，表示准确

（125）understand see get grasp comprehend 理解

understand：懂；理解；领会

see：明白

get：（口语）懂（笑话、描述）

grasp：理解（事实 技能、想法）

comprehend：理解、领悟（比较正式）

以上这些近义词汇虽非详解，却可以帮助读者简单快速地掌握和理解近义词间的细微差别，起到化繁为简、四两拨千斤的作用。词汇永远是翻译过程中最重要的一环，如何在双向的翻译中准确、优美、传神地使用词汇是我们永远共同面对的挑战。

第三章　翻译的语法观

英文的语法与中文的语法有很大的不同,一个"外紧"一个"内松"。"外紧"的英文语法习惯于将语义呈现在表面,用更多细节的顺序和各种功能词的安排来充分表达语义,而不趋向留下空间让读者或听者去思考,以避免模棱两可的表达。句子、短语等结构的使用更加严谨和考究,以便能以最准确的方式来表达语义。"内松"的中文语法方便语义的内在传递,即更多得让读者或听者去体会、感受和分析作者的真实语义。本章试图通过探讨英文语法的一些特点,来诠释如何正确地使用语法规则来准确灵活表达我们的语义。

第一节　主语的设置

汉语经常用"有生命"的事物作主语,英文体现"万物皆有灵"的理念,亦常用"无生命"的事物作主语。因此在翻译时,我们经常要考虑将汉语和英语的主语进行改变,以便更地道进行"里译"和"外译"的表达。比如:"我喜欢音乐"除译为 I love music 之外,我们亦可译作：Music is my favorite. "我有了一个绝佳的想法"可译为：A great idea pops up in my mind.

第二节　主动与被动

英文主被动语态出现频率远高于汉语，特别是表达主观情感情绪的词汇，如：interest, excite, fascinate, thrill, amaze 等。这些词的主被动有时会让我们瞬间不知如何转译。如果我们转换一下思维，将"主动"理解为"情感来源"（source of feeling），将"被动"理解为"情感体验者"（experiencer）可能会更好地帮助我们区分主被动关系。例如：若我们内心产生一种情绪（excitement），我们要找到这种情绪从何而来，比如源自某条新闻，那这条新闻就是这种情绪的来源，也就是主动一方，就用 exciting 来表述；而我们正在体会这种情绪，因此我们是体验人，也就是被动一方，用 excited 来表述。

第三节　及物与不及物

英文中的动词有及物和不及物动词之分，其中及物动词占动词总量比例大约 60%，不及物动词占比 20%，可以兼作及物和不及物的动词占比 20%。及物与不及物之分主要是源于能不能及物或有没有必要强调其及物的属性。比如 we look at each other. 这里的 look 表现我们的眼睛，因此，它是不能和"看"的对象零距离的，所以要用"at"这个介词表现出眼睛与视觉对象之间的距离感。而 see 是我们的目光，所以必须是及物的，目之所及才能看到。再有 smile at 也是同理，我们微笑的表情一定与微笑的对象有距离。在既可及物又可不及物的动词方面，也体现出"距离感"这一概念。例如：Mark is flying the plane. 此表达可凸显其娴熟的驾驶技术。Mark is flying in the plane. 介词"in"表现了 Mark 和 plane 之间的距离，没有达到人机合一。再如：The girl is riding the horse. 此句传递了其马术精湛之意。而 The girl is riding on the horse. 介词 on 将骑马者的 "不从容"体现出来。简言之：概念距离（conceptual distance）可借由语言距离（linguistic distance）来传达，即通过介词的使用与否来具体表述。

第四节　冠　词

在任意一篇英语文章中，冠词所占比例都高达 10%，因此，虽然冠词不是实词，但由于其出现频率高，加之又有很强的语法功能，所以准确使用冠词是一位好译者的必备技能。一般来说，我们不会在不定冠词上出问题，但定冠词往往是个挑战。根据《大学英语语法》一书的分类，定冠词有 59 种使用方法，但仔细分析发现，实际上真正影响我们翻译质量的就是定冠词的 "特指"功能。即我们第二次提到某人某物时，要用定冠词来说明这是刚刚提到的对象。如：Two women met at the entrance of a grocery. The first woman brought a child with her. The child took something from the shelf... 在这段话中，出现了四次定冠词 the，分别体现了定冠词的四种用法：第一个定冠词表示 "特指" grocery 的 entrance。因先前句中提到两个 women，所以第二次提到其中一人时，单用一个定冠词 the 无法区分二人，而用 the first（double determiner）。The child 因为第二次提到孩子，特指这个孩子。而最后的 shelf 是第一次提到，却也使用了 the，这又是为什么呢？因为这属于常识，grocery 必有货架，因此即便第一次提到，也要用定冠词。笔者注意到英语定冠词的使用习惯：当我们描述比较熟悉的地点时，习惯性地少用定冠词；反之描述相对陌生的地点则多用定冠词，因为前者已经熟悉到不用特指的程度，而后者则需要特殊说明一下。

第五节　时态的另一面

英语时态一直是英语学习者非常重视且倍感纠结的语法问题。我们来看几个例句：

Yesterday my landlord tells me my rent is going up.

昨天房东告诉我房租要涨价。

Tomorrow I fly to London for a big meeting.

明天我要飞伦敦开个重要会议。

Today I woke up with a headache.

我今早醒来时头疼。

以上几句都是摘自原版英文书，明明是"昨天"却用一般现在时，"明天"也用一般现在时，而"今天"却用一般过去时。似乎英语母语者不在乎时态的束缚。而真实的情况是，"现在时态""过去时态"除了表达时间概念，还可以表达距离概念。"现在时"可表距离较近（或可能性较大）；"过去时"可表示距离较远（或可能性较小）；而"将来时态"则可表示一种可能性。这就解释了为什么我们对陌生人、长辈、领导或老板说话时要用 would you，could you 这样的委婉语，因为过去式的 would、could 比现在时的 will、can 更能表达出与谈话对象的心理距离，这种距离感体现出尊重。同理，当我们预测未来时，可以通过选择使用 may 或者 might 来区分表达我们对自己的预测有多大的把握。在请求帮助时，可依据所需帮助的难度来决定用 can you 还是 could you。

第六节　条件句

对英语时态的新角度认知后，我们来分析另一个难点——条件句。严格来讲，所有未来都是假定的，因为不论可能性多大，只要没发生就是不确定的，即有"虚拟"的成分在，并且往往与一定的条件相连。前面讲到，"过去时态"除了表达时间概念外，还可表达距离概念(可能性大则距离近,可能性小则距离远。)这样的解读在应用到理解条件句时同样适用。我们可以把条件句分为四个层次:可能性较大、可能性 50%、可能性小,和没有可能性。这 4 个层次的条件句分别用如下方式表述:

If you need something you just buy it.

若你需要什么,买就行了。(用一般现在时,实现可能性极大。)

If you ask John, he will help you.

如果你求约翰,他会帮你的。(现在时＋将来时,实现可能 50% 左右。)

If you asked John, he would help you。

如果你求约翰,他应该会帮你。(两个过去时态,可能性相对较小。)

If you had asked John, he would have helped you.

如果当时你求了约翰,他可能就帮你了。(虚拟语气——在假设一种不可能改变的过去)

第七节　情态动词

英文的几个情态动词 will can may must should 都有与之相对应的实意短语:

Will – be going to

Can – be able to

May – be allowed to

Must – have to

Should – be supposed to

个人认为情态动词偏向体现笔者或发言人的主观意念,表达情绪意愿时可多用情态动词,但其说服力弱。若要使自己的表述更显客观,则用实意动词更好。所以当我们在叙述一件事情时,应更多使用实词性质的表达。这也是为什么 must 在英语中出现频率很低,因为有主观强迫命令别人的感觉,而 have to 则更强调客观状况,有替对方着想的意味,因而也更容易被接受。

第八节 介 词

下面说说功能词——介词的一些妙用。介词在英语中的使用率远高于汉语,这与英语注重句子结构的严谨和细致有关。英文最基本的表示位置的介词是, at, on, in。at 表示在一个"点"; on 表示在一个面或一条线上; 而 in 表示在一个立体当中。从一点到另一点用 from to; 从一个面到另一个面 off … onto; 从一个立体到另一个立体 out of … into; 经过一个点用 past; 经过一个面或一条线用 along; 经过一个立体用 through。掌握了这些基本认知,我们就可以活用介词,妙笔生花,特别是在表达抽象事物时。举几个实例:

I'm in love; I'm in difficulty; I'm in trouble(沉浸其中的感受,所以用 in)。

I'm in it.(表示我们正在经历一件事)

I'm on it.(代表事情在你的掌控之下)

I am writing a paper.(客观表述)

I am writing through a paper.(更具挑战意味)

第九节 动副词组

相较于动 + 介词组,动 + 副词组更被视为是一个整体,因有时很难单纯从字面猜出其真实含义,所以往往容易给我们记忆带来麻烦。笔者发现使用最多的是 up, down, on, off, out, away 这几个副词,其使用频率占所有使用比例的60%以上。由此可见,如果我们能掌握这几个副词在词组中的隐含语义,则解决了大部分动副词组的语义问题。下面我们一一对这几个高频副词在词组中的语义进行分析。

up 作为副词的基本含义是"向上",如 climb up(爬上), go up(上去), shoot up(快速生长); 但在另一些动副词组中,如:

turn up，fire up，drink up，beat up，stir up 等并没有 "向上" 的
"方向性" 含义，而是 "增加" 这个共同语义。turn up 是 "可见度"
的增加；fire up 是 "情绪" 的增加；beat up 是 "伤害程度" 的增加；
drink up 是 "量" 的增加等。

而 "down" 与之相反，即减少、降低。例如：calm down 是 "情
绪" 的降低，slow down 是 "速度" 的降低。

副词 on 的基本含义是 "接触"，比如 turn on the TV 表示 "电
路" 的接触，put on clothes 表示 "衣服和身体" 的接触，go on 表
示 "保持" 接触状态。

off，则表示从 "接触" 到 "离开" 的语义。例如 take off your
clothes，衣物 "离开" 身体；turn off the computer 电路被切断；
put off the meeting 时间被取消。

副词 out 除了表示基本的 "从里到外" 的含义，还有这样一
些词组：put out，knock out，fill out，burn out，它们的共同点是
都带有某种 "变化" 的含义。put out fire 从燃烧到熄灭的变化；
knock out 从清醒到昏迷的变化；fill out the form 从空白到信息
完整的变化；burn out 从燃烧到熄灭。

away 的基本含义是 "离开"，比如：kick away（踢开），walk
away（走开），put away（拿开）。但有些词组如：carry away，
chat away 等，这些词组的共同含义是 "没完没了"，因此 carried
away by music 表达的是余音绕梁，chat away 喋喋不休的闲谈。
甚至我们可以利用这一规则来大胆创造出属于自己的词组，比
如：write away，长时间地写作；fight away 坚持不断地战斗等。

第十节　直接、间接宾语

请看下面的例句：

He described the picture to us. 正确

He described us the picture. 错误

It costs me a lot of money. 正确

It costs a lot of money to me. 错误

一般将"人"作为间接宾语,将"物"作为直接宾语,我们先接触物再接触人。例:I give him some new books. 我是先拿到书,然后才送给人,但句子的顺序是"先人后物"。另一个解读角度是,当接受人成为物品的新主人,我们通常会将人放在前面。另一种情况是,如果接受方是个地点,则将直接宾语放在后面(介词的后面)。例:The Red Cross sent relief supplies to Rwanda.(红十字会给卢旺达送去援助物资。)这里卢旺达是个地点,因此虽然是直接宾语,但放在介词的后面。

在宣布(announce)、声称(declare)、描述(describe)、解释(explain)、报告(report)等谓语之后通常将"内容"放在前面,将"人"放在后面,因为这时候的"人"是接受方,并不是内容的所有人。例如:We reported the results to the crowd.(我们将结果报告给大家。)

They explain the plan to the committee.(我们向委员会解释了计划)。

在沟通类的谓语动词之后,往往间接宾语的"人"放在介词后面。例如:say/shout/scream/murmur/whisper something to someone,而不是 say/shout/scream/murmur/whisper someone something。

如果谓语动词不会给作为宾语的"人"带来变化,则将人放在介词后面作间接宾语;反之则将"人"放在谓语动词的后面。

例如:The loud music gives me a terrible headache.(头疼的"变化")

These grammar lessons give me pain in the neck.(心情的"变化")

基于同样道理,下面的句子也将"人"作为间接宾语放到谓语的后面:

The deal costs me a fortune.(经济状况的"变化")

The police fined him fifty yuan.(钱财的"变化")

直接和间接宾语位置安排的另一个考虑是"前旧后新"。看一下例句:I give some money to Jack.(可能已经给了其他人钱,可以理解钱为"旧")。I give Jack some money.(可能已经给杰克其他东西了,可以视杰克为"旧"。)

直接宾语和间接宾语位置的最后一个考量是"前短后长"。

例：He handed her a large brown envelope.

直接宾语 a large brown envelope 相比间接宾语 her 较长，所以放在后面。

第十一节　尾部重量

英语中的并列句、并列词组或并列单词，习惯上是将比较长的部分放在后面，也就是"前短后长"，这种现象叫作"尾部重量"（end weight）。例如：

If I were you, I wouldn't take his words for granted.

You would be hurt if you had heard what he had said behind you.

将两句进行比较，我们发现条件句和主句的位置因长短的不同而位置不同。其他类似句子：原因从句、转折句、对比句等亦如此，甚至英语后置定语也是源于这样的语言习惯而做出安排的。

第四章　翻译技巧

经过上一章我们对语法进行了一些多维度的理解后，这一章将以大量的例句来为大家介绍一些翻译上的实用技巧。

第一节　长定语的翻译

英语的长定语包括从句、独立结构等，较之汉语的定语有位置、使用方式、使用频率方面的不同，所以长定语的翻译一直是我们英语学习中的难点。整个高三英语语法大都围绕定语从句和长定语展开。我们学习外语，不可避免地会以母语作为参照，因此外语学习的过程就是摆脱母语干扰的过程。在翻译比较复杂的语言文字时，大脑需在两个语言频道间频繁转换，由于对母语本就自然依赖，此时大脑更容易受母语影响，而长定语翻译的困难之处正在于此。

在翻译实践中，根据原句的特点和句子长短，可尝试运用两种翻译技巧：

原句较短，可译成标准的汉语定语句式。

例：Besides coffee industry, there are many other fields in

which Uganda and China can cooperate.

译文：除咖啡产业外，乌中之间在很多其他领域都可开展合作。

原句较长，可将定语从句拆开单译。

例：After years of economic reform, this country has achieved macro-economic stability characterized by low inflation, stable exchange rates and consistently high economic growth.

参考译文：经过数年的经济改革，这个国家实现了以低通胀、汇率稳定和持续高速的经济增长为特点的宏观经济的稳定。

较佳译文：经过数年经济改革，这个国家实现了宏观经济的稳定，其特点为低通胀、汇率稳定和持续高速的经济增长。

因为在即时口译翻译中，时间有限，若译成较长的句子，容易产生口误或错误，导致听者理解困难。汉译英时更要注意长定语的翻译，毕竟我们英语的使用不如汉语熟练，如果在长句翻译中稍有语法错误就会影响翻译质量。英文母语使用者的第一追求是意思的清晰明了，而不是句式和用词的复杂华丽。

第二节　无主句的翻译

无主句是汉语使用中常出现的情况。

例：医院将提升学术水平作为重中之重，实施科研精品战略，以立足长远、收缩战线、调整布局、突出重点、加强协作、结合医疗为方针，加强学科建设、重点实验室和科研队伍建设，先后培养出 5 个国家重点学科，18 个省重点学科，8 个卫生部重点实验室，为获取重大科研课题和重大科研成果奠定了基础。

在这样一个长句中只有开头一个主语。翻译中如果也这样设计句子结构，就会产生非常混乱的感觉。建议具体翻译方案如下：

添加主语：The hospital prioritizes the upgrading of academic capacity and establishment of key disciplines. It practices the "Strategy of Premium Research". It holds on to the Long-term based, concentrated, restructured and concerted guideline which combines with medical service.

被动语态: Key disciplines and key labs are emphasized in the process which resulted in the establishment of 5 national level disciplines, 18 provincial ones and 8 labs of ministerial importance.

在书面和非常正式的场合可用从句: That premium research is practiced as a strategy, that the guideline of long-term, concentrated, prioritized development are emphasized.

第三节　替代词的使用

在我们阅读翻译作品时,常感文字表述不顺,很重要的一个原因是,英文替代词的使用要远多于汉语。其中包括代词、名词、助动词、系动词等。此时,我们应该注意依照目标语言的使用习惯进行转译。

例 1: 沈阳是个以制造业为经济基础的城市, ⋯ ⋯, 沈阳还是个有着上千年历史的古城。

译文: Shenyang is a manufacturing based industrial city ..., it is also a thousand years old ancient city.

例 2: The secretary of Defense and the Secretary of State made similar statements in several occasions, the latter made it in a more diplomatic way.

译文: 国防部长和国务卿都就此事在若干场合发表了相似言论,国务卿的讲话更显官方。

例 3: I prefer cars made in Germany to those made in Japan.

译文: 相比日本汽车,我更喜欢德国车。

另一种替代是用可表示其特点的名词替代。

例: Both China and the United States are great countries in the world and their partnership will be contributive to world peace and development. <u>The greatest development country and the greatest developing country</u> will certainly play leverage in world affairs.

译文：中美两个大国及其伙伴关系会对世界和平和发展做出巨大贡献，两国在世界事务中将起到举足轻重的作用。

注：英文表述中分别用表示各自特点的名词 the greatest developed country 和 the greatest developing country 替代各自的名称。这样的情况在英文中比比皆是。如提及中国时可用 the fastest growing economy；the most populous country in the world；the ancient oriental civilization 等。提到美国时可用 the most advance economy；the only superpower 等。

助动词、系动词替代

例 1：The climate of Yellow Mountains changes vertically, <u>so does</u> the flora.

译文：黄山的气候呈垂直变化，植物<u>也是</u>垂直变化分布。

例 2：The Japanese are concerned about the bilateral relationship, <u>so are the</u> Chinese.

译文：日本人关心双边关系，中国人<u>同样关心</u>。

第四节　尾　重

翻译的过程实际也是总结两个语言特点，并准确加以利用，以达到标准地道的过程。在英文中，常会出现以下这样的从句：

India's biggest-ever financial scandal shook the Bombay Stock Exchange in April *as a long bull market on the exchange ended amid allegations of insider trading, stock manipulation, and illegal diversion of bank depositor's funds.*

Italy's leading anti-Mafia fighter, Judge Giovanni Falcone, his wife and three bodyguards were killed *when a massive bomb detonated on an expressway where he and his family were driving.*

As South Africa stumbled toward a multiracial society, a number of scandals involving that nation's police and security forces rocked the government of President De Klerk.

The ceremony would take place on time *if the weather and the other surrounding elements will turn up well*

If he will be available, the opening ceremony will take place on time.

从上述斜体从句的表达可见,从句若长于主句则放在前面,否则放在后面。这种习惯被称为 End Weight,在翻译中应注意,以达到地道的翻译效果。

第五节　三段式翻译

中文表述中常出现多谓语情况。

例 1:大连地处辽东半岛南端,风光美丽宜人,是东北乃至东北亚地区重要的海港城市。

注:这种情况下,建议将次要谓语译为独立结构,另两个谓语译为双谓语句子。

译文: Situated on the south tip of Lidong Peninsula, Dalian is a city of pleasantry and a harbor city of regional importance in Northeast China, even in Northeast Asia.

例 2:××说:体育健儿参加世界大赛,就是为力争第一,就是要争取升国旗、奏国歌,为国争光。

注:如有超过四个谓语的长句子,建议把它译为两句话,以免造成语法表达上的混乱

译文: Participating international sports events, athletes are eager to have their national flag hoisted, national anthem played, to top the competitors and to gain glory for their motherland.

较佳译文: Participating international sports events, athletes are eager to have their national flag hoisted, national anthem played. They have a desire to top the competitors and to gain glory for their motherland.

第六节　插入语

英文会使用很多插入语,跟汉语相比这是较为独特的现象,在翻译中应该注意句子成分位置的变化,以达到更加地道的语言表述效果。

例 1: Another impediment to archeological research, <u>one of world wide concern</u>, was the increasing resistance to excavation of the remains of indigenous inhabitants.

译文:<u>令世界关注的</u>另一个对考古研究的阻碍是人们对当地居民遗产的发掘的抵制。

例 2: Writing well, <u>as opposed to speaking well</u>, requires an understanding of the breakdown of technical skills into specific order.

译文:<u>与口语不同的是</u>,写作要求理解将技巧分解成具体的顺序。

例 3: The outcome, <u>one hopes</u>, results in an increase in knowledge.

译文:<u>有人希望</u>其结果会是知识的增加。

例 4: There was one thing, <u>however</u>, that Ben couldn't seem to conquer

译文:<u>但是</u>,有一个本杰明无法征服的东西。

例 5: But there was no way, <u>other than the name Michael</u>, that the owner could be identified.

译文:<u>但除了迈克尔这个名字外</u>,没有办法能确认主任是谁。

例 6: She went, <u>on April 20th</u>, to the place she had been dreamed of for so long.

译文:<u>4 月 20 日</u>,她去了那个她梦想很久的地方。

例 7: Zookeepers know, <u>to their despair</u>, that many species of animals will not bread with just any other animal of their species.

译文:<u>令他们失望的是</u>,动物饲养员知道很多动物并不随意与同类交配。

第七节　句子成分转换

一些经验不足的译者往往进行字对字的翻译，经常费力不讨好，且译出的语言文字显得不伦不类，有时甚至令人费解。实际上翻译是一个思想传递的过程，而非一味追求语言的绝对忠实。

例1：装备制造业是国家工业化、现代化的标志，也是国民经济的基础，是一个国家竞争力的体现。

译文：Capacity of Equipment manufacturing indicates industrialization and modernization, underlies national economy and backs up national competitiveness.

注：将原文的宾语译成谓语。

例2：短短两个小时的演讲中，各位专家围绕信息化和先进技术的主题畅所欲言。

译文：Two hours are too short for the frank utterance made by our speakers on the subject of informationization and advance technology.

注：将原文的时间状语译为主语。

例3：春天，盛开的鲜花色彩缤纷，点缀山坡；夏天可以看到青翠的山峰一座连着一座，秋天把整个黄山装扮成红紫相间的世界；冬天，到处是银石银枝。

译文：Spring sees flowers in riot of colors, dotting the expanse of slop; you will see hill upon hill of green with streams giggling midst them; Autumn dresses the mountains into a world of purple and blazing red; in winter silver rocks and boughs spreading the whole scene.

注：把时间状语译为主语。

例4：从那以后，燕京大学这所外国教会学校发生很大变化，它逐渐成为完全由中国人自己掌握的学校。

译文：Thereafter, transformation took place in Yanjing University, the foreign missionary institution and it gradually fell back to

Chinese hand.

注：把宾语译为主语

例 5：随着世界科技的发展，新华社的通信技术已基本实现现代化。

译文：World's technological progress enables the modernization of ICT of Xinhua.

注：把状语译为主语。

第八节　填词、省略法

在翻译过程中，原则上不能随意加词，但为更好地表达，以便读者或听者更好地理解，翻译时也可添加词，前提是虽原文中未提及，但明显隐含其意。

例 1：Without your help, my trip to China wouldn't have been such a pleasant one.

译文：如果没有你的帮助，我的中国之行不会如此愉快。

例 2：She is good at singing and painting.

译文：她很善唱歌和画画。

有添，就有略，两者都是由文化差异、语言习惯造成的。如果不进行必要的处理，自然无法达到最佳翻译效果。

例 1：This is the pen he always writes with.

译文：这是他常写字的笔。

注：省略了 the，that，with

例 2：会议讨论了环保问题。

译文：Meeting discussed environmental protection.

注：省略了"问题"。

例 3：I'll inform you the latest once I got it.

译文：得到最新消息我就告诉你。

注：省略了 it。

英语中连词的使用量很大，很多情况下都可以不译。

例 1：It's getting wet outside, so let's take our umbrella.

译文：外面下雨，我们拿上伞吧。

注：省略连词 so。

例 2：Since it's dinner time now, I'll take you to a nearby restaurant.

译文：到晚饭时间了，我带你们去附近的饭店。

注：省略连词 since。

第九节　分类使用词汇

在第二章"如何成为词汇大师"的第五节中我们探讨了单词的分类记忆与使用，接下来的部分，我们通过更多例子来进一步学习。

例 1：由于两国关系的特殊性，对来访者，一定要隆重的欢迎。

译文：Consider the relation between the two nations, we should roll out the red carpet for each other's visitors.

注：用 roll out the red carpet 来替代 welcome 的含义，非常有画面感。

例 2：One of the flaws of the One-Child policy is that the parents try to build walls around their children, instead of having them to face challenges themselves.

译文：独生子女政策的弊端之一是家长为孩子提供了全方位的保护，而不让他们独自面对挑战。

注：用 build walls around 来表达保护，用比喻的效果更好。

例 3：Nobody could dissuade him from taking the risk, all we can do is to cross our fingers to him.

译文：没有人能劝说他放弃冒险，就只能祝他好运喽！

注：用 cross fingers to sb. 表达 wish good luck 的意思，非常生动。

例 4：求知是一个人的优点，而窥探隐私则是缺点。

译文：It is good to be curious, but negative to be inquisitive.

注：用褒义词 curious 和一个贬义词 inquisitive 去对比，句

子结构工整且有对比感。

例 5: In a partnership like theirs, one of them does the brainwork while the other the muscle-work.

译文: 他们之间的合作模式是,一个人用脑,另一个人执行。

注: 用 brainwork 和 muscle-work 去形容脑力和体力很匹配且押韵。

第十节　动名词的翻译

do some cleaning 译为打扫卫生。而英文字面的意思是做一些清扫。因此 do some cleaning 不应被视为短语,而是随意使用的一个结构。我们把 some 去掉,变成 do cleaning 其意思不变,等于是我们在翻译时加了一个宾语,使之更符合汉语习惯,减少翻译痕迹。同样的例子还有很多,如: do some washing——洗衣服, do some reading——读书等。类似的表达还有: do shopping, do cooking, do gardening, do sewing 等。翻译这种英文的技巧就是为其添加宾语,上述表达就译为"购物,做饭,侍弄花园,做针线活"等。

第十一节　减译法

由于英汉两种语言的语法结构、表达方式以及修辞风格不同,有些词语或句子成分在英语中是必不可少的,但若原封不动搬入汉语,就会影响译文的简洁和通顺。因此在英译汉的过程中,为了简化译文,需要省略一些可有可无或翻译后感觉累赘的词语。但必须注意,减译不等于直接删除。

1. 省略代词

例 1: We are pleased to have received your invitation to the symposium on internet.

译文: 非常高兴收到你寄来的参加互联网大会的邀请。

注：省略 we。

例 2：If the chain reaction went on without being checked, it could cause a terrible explosion.

译文：如果连锁反应不加控制，就可能引发可怕的爆炸。

注：省略代词 it。

例 3：There are many kinds of welding materials, we can classify them according to their characteristics.

译文：有很多种焊接材料，我们可以按特点分类

注：省略代词 their。

2.省略冠词

例：The volume of a gas increase more quickly than that of a liquid.

译文：气体体积增加的速度比液体快。

注：省略冠词 a。

3.省略连词

例：When the pressure gets low, the boiling-point become low.

译文：气压低，沸点就低。

注：省略连词 when。

4.省略介词

例：Over the years, tools and technology themselves as a source of fundamental innovation have largely been ignored by historian and philosophers of science.

译文：多年来，工具和技术本身作为根本性的创新源泉，在很大程度上被科学史学家和科学哲学家忽视。

注：省略介词 over。

5.省略名词

例：Perhaps you have overlooked the fact that your account for May purchases has not yet been settled.

译文：也许你忘记了五月份购物贷款还没有结算。

注：省略名词 account。

6. 省略动词

例：There is no doubt that we'll carry out the experiment successfully.

译文：毫无疑问我们一定能把实验搞成功。

注：省略 there is。

第五章　习惯用语翻译

在翻译活动中,我们会碰到大量"习语类"或"中国传统文化类"的翻译内容,这对于任何一个翻译人员来说都是一个挑战。习语类的语言具有以下特点:

(1)言简意赅。习语,无论在英语还是汉语中都是语言精华。

(2)意义深刻。例如成语包含深刻的人生哲理,能起到警醒和建议作用。

(3)广为流传。比如我们可以通过使用成语,用较少的文字来阐述复杂深奥的语义,达到事半功倍的效果。

英语中 idiom 一词,包含了汉语中的成语、俗语、谚语、歇后语等特色语言。中文将 idiom 一词译成"习语",这个词几乎是为 idiom 特意创造的汉语词汇。

由于习语的特殊性,我们在翻译时必定要用相对比较特殊的方式来翻译,以便让读者/听者感受到这个"表达法"的特别之处。英译汉时,我们作为母语为汉语的使用者,能够更自如地用比较考究的方式将英文习语译成中文,例如直译法,即英文习语可以找到与之意思契合的汉语。比如:

Love me love my dog.

爱屋及乌。

Great minds think alike.

英雄所见略同。

Man proposes, God disposes.

尽人事听天命。

即便是英文的一些习语无法找到非常合适的成语，我们也能轻松地以某种方式将其译成"短小精悍"的汉语文本。因此接下来将重点介绍汉语习语译成英文的技巧。

第一节　押韵法

英语有压头韵(alliteration)和压尾韵(rhyme)两种押韵，请看例子：

一、压头韵

压头韵是两个单词或两个词组的首字母相同，可以是元音也可以是辅音字母。例如：

bread and butter 基本生活所需

Cut and carve 精练

Forgive and forget 不念旧恶

Friend and foe 敌友

Safe and sound 平安无事

Time and tide 岁月

Facts and figures 事实数据

Beauty and beast 美女与野兽

Fame and fortune 名利

Sense and sensibility 理智与情感

下面是 1912 年美国沃伦哈丁在共和党大会上讲话的节选：

Progress is not proclamation nor palaver. It is not pretense nor play on prejudice. It is not personal pronouns, nor perennial pronouncement. It is not the perturbation of people's passion-wrought, no promise proposed.

　　进步既不是宣言书也不是空话；既不是伪善也不是玩弄偏见；不代表某个个体，也不是长年的口头承诺；它不惧怕人们激情燃烧，也不仅仅是简单的承诺。

　　我们看到其中用了大量的压头韵单词来增加说话的韵律和力量。

　　再来看一则交通安全警示语：

Careless cars cutting corners create confusion.

Crossing centerlines.

Countless collisions cost coffins.

Copy?

Continue cautiously !

Comply?

Cool.

　　莽撞司机抄近路，引发交通混乱。

　　不遵守规则，造成无数伤亡。

　　醒醒吧，还是安全驾驶吧！

　　明白？

　　棒棒哒！

　　大量字母 C 开头单词的使用形成了压头韵，从而使得这段交通警示变得更加有趣且朗朗上口。

　　再来欣赏一则沃特尼啤酒的广告词：

What we want is Watney's.

　　我们都要沃特尼。

　　并不出彩的一句广告词，但因用了压头韵的技法使其变得不俗气且能够产生共鸣。

二、压尾韵

　　压尾韵的原则是结尾元音相同。请看例子：

Once I had a strange nightmare,

I dreamt of an electric chair,

I sat in it and said a prayer,

And I woke up with curly hair.

一次我做了个奇怪的梦，

梦见自己坐上了电椅，

我坐在上面，内心祈祷，

醒来时头发直直竖起。

每句最后一个单词都是押韵的：nightmare，chair，prayer，hair。

再来看则童谣：

Humpty dumpty sat on the wall

Humpty dumpty had a great fall

小胖墩坐墙头，一不小心摔下了。

与中文童谣一样，英语中大量儿歌也都是以押韵的形式呈现，笔者称其为早期的 rap，韵律十足，朗朗上口，极有感染力。

下面是一则农谚：

Corn's knee high, June or July.

六月七月，玉米及膝。

再来看首幽默的打油诗：

I don't like dentist，because they hurt me，

With horrid bad pinchers as sharp as can be，

They pick at my teeth and scratch in my head，

Until I begin to wish I were dead.

But I read in the pater（so I suppose it's so），

That all of the dentists to heaven will go，

Because they are needed a way up there，

To make gold crown for the angels' fair.

我不喜欢牙医，因为他们折磨我，

手握尖利无比的可怕钳子，

捅在我牙，痛在我心，

简直生不如死。

我在报上读到，所以那一定是真的，

所有牙医都会升天，

去为天使的舞会准备金王冠。

在我们了解了押韵法的基本规则之后，我们就可以有的放矢

地进行一些翻译实践了。

例 1：买卖兴隆通四海，财源茂盛达三江。

译文：Business is thriving, reaching out to the five continents, Profit is recurring from four oceans of the planet.

（thriving 和 recurring 押韵。）

例 2：散装集装绝无野蛮装运

车队船队保证安全迅速

译文：Bulk or container stowing, absolutely free of rough handling, Marine vehicle fleet, definitely guaranteed safety and speed.

（stowing 和 handling 押韵，fleet 和 speed 押韵。）

例 3：

要买房 到建行

译文：Wanna buy a house but financially scant,

Why not come to construction bank.

（Scant 和 bank 押韵。）

例 4：要想皮肤好 天天用大宝

译文：Applying Dabao morning and night,

Making skincare a real delight.

（Night 和 delight 押韵。）

例 5：海上生明月 天涯共此时

译文：The bright moon rises over the sea,

We share its beauty with thee.

（sea 和 thee 押韵。）

在一些较难找到押韵词的翻译中，可以通过前缀和后缀押韵来实现。例如这句："优良品质，优惠价格，优质服务"。我们很难找到三个既押韵又可准确表达优良、优惠和优质的单词，但通过加前缀，我们就能做到了：unrivaled quality, unbeaten price, unreserved service.

第二节　对比法

"押韵法"不是万能钥匙，它只是习语翻译的方法之一，我们需要"因地制宜",比如用"对比法"。

先看一些例子：

例1：比上不足，比下有余

译文：worse off than some，better off than many

例2：内忧外患

译文：trouble within，threat without

例3：少壮不努力 老大徒伤悲

译文：a lazy youth a lousy age

例4：今天是老百姓扬眉吐气的一天。

译文：It is a big day for the small people.

例5：他是个正直爽快的人。

译文：He is upright and outright.

例6：避暑好去处。（旅行社广告语）

译文：It a cool place on a hot day.

例7：对于平凡人这是不平凡的事。

译文：It is unusual for the usual.

例8：这是个网红酒吧。

译文：It's a hot spot for cool cats

通过这些例子可以看到，用"对比法"翻译一些习语也是非常好的，我们尽可大胆地去实践。

第三节　特殊结构法

我们一定会遇到用"押韵法"和"对比法"都无法解决的习语翻译问题，那么还有个屡试不爽的，可以满足习语翻译基本要求，即让人感觉到其特殊性的方法，那就是特殊结构法。

请看例子：

例1：Bright forecast for futures market.

译文：市场前景一片大好。

例2：Changing on course to be country's shipbuilding capital.

译文：国家造船之都，打造进行时。

例 3：Park to become national materials center.

译文：工业园将成为国家物资中心。

例 4：Air force no threat to others.

译文：空军不会对任何人形成威胁。

例 5：Father of China's space program mourned.

译文：悼念中国航天之父。

例 6：Forum on sky safety.

译文：天空安全论坛启动。

例 7：Water tech forum to begin.

译文：水科技论坛即将开始。

例 8：Fish killed in lake pollution.

译文：湖泊污染造成死鱼成群。

例 9：Food for thought.

译文：发人深省的事件 / 精神食粮。

如果大家对上面的表达进行分析就会发现，它们都没有谓语，都不是完整的句子，这就是特殊结构。有的是独立主格，有的是短语和独立结构等。只要我们把一个句子的谓语去掉，就会得到各种特殊结构，在使表达变得简单的同时，又不失语义的完整。可以被视为是非常"救急"的一个习语翻译方式。

阅读是提高语言能力最主要的手段和最有效的途径，有针对性的高质量阅读更是快速提高专业领域能力的"捷径"。在接下来的几章中，笔者按主题分类整理了一些文字素材供大家阅读、学习并应用实践。翻译是个二次创作的过程，不存在唯一版本或绝对正确，因此笔者并未附上所谓的"正确答案"，而是为大家提供了重点词汇、难点句的翻译参考，请大家视接下来的几章内容为"实战"挑战，披荆斩棘，开启你的翻译征程吧。

第六章 文 化

范文 1

词汇 Vocabulary

legion 同类人群

humanity 人道

exploit 功绩

icon 偶像

samaritan 英国慈善团体撒马利亚会

atruism 利他主义

pique 引起兴趣或好奇

fire up 动员；鼓劲儿

private 列兵

souvenir 纪念品

posters 海报；宣传画

UNICEF 联合国儿童基金会

roaming 漫游

leukemia 白血病

plumber 下水道工

wane 衰败

revere 敬重

Leif Rogers, an American living in Liaoning province, is among the legions of enthusiastic admirers of Lei Feng, one of China's most famous soldiers, renowned not for his battlefield exploits but his humanity.

Lei Feng (1940—1962) became a New China icon in the 1960s for his charitable deeds and good Samaritan altruism, and his legend grew after his sudden death in an accident.

For decades, the young soldier was a role model for an entire generation.

Rogers first discovered the legend of Lei Feng on a hot summer night in 2005.

On his first visit to China, Rogers walked out of the Beijing Capital International Airport and hopped in a cab and the driver asked his name.

"Leif", Rogers replied.

"Lei Feng! Your name is so close to Lei Feng." the driver exclaimed.

Rogers didn't learn much about the model soldier during the ride because of the language barrier but the admiring expression on the driver's face when he referred to Lei Feng piqued his curiosity, which was already fired up by his journey to China.

Rogers' first job was teaching journalism at Liaoning University of Technology in Jinzhou. He discovered this was the same city where Lei Feng served in the army. Locals there continue to revere the soldier.

With the assistance of his colleagues and students, the American collected many stories and pictures of Lei Feng and his knowledge grew.

"Most of the military heroes I know are remembered for their performances in battles," he says. "While Lei Feng, the most distinguished soldier in China, was just a common private who drove a truck. That is why I was so attracted to him."

Customers to Roger's office are amazed at the special glass cabinet, where he has placed most of his precious collections of Lei Feng.

The display includes a white ceramic statue, which he treasures the most, calendars, cups, matchboxes and other souvenirs with political posters of Lei Feng.

Rogers has also added his own work to the collection by translating a book of Lei Feng's quotes.

"A student at university gave me the *Dairies of Lei Feng* in 2006," he says.

"It is in Chinese and my Chinese was very limited. And I couldn't find an English version. There was very limited English information about Lei Feng so I thought I should do something on my part."

In 2007, he published a book *Learn from Comrade Lei Feng* which he distributes to people wherever he goes.

"What I most appreciate in Lei Feng is his being so humble after doing good deeds," he says.

"That makes a comparison today as so much is about who you are and how much you are recognized."

Lei Feng's anecdotes also reminded Rogers of his late father, who once worked in Africa and Papua New Guinea for UNICEF. He traveled with his roaming parents and discovered the highest virtue in life was to serve his fellow men.

Rogers found this same selfless spirit in Lei Feng and himself volunteers to aid others, including visiting orphans and raising funds for a leukemia-stricken girl.

He also looks for other ways to try a little kindness. Two years ago, a local family came to Rogers's office for help. They had lost contact with their 19-year-old son, who was studying in Los Angeles.

"I stayed up all night on the phone talking to my friends in

LA," he says. "We finally tracked the boy down three days later. He moved out of his apartment without telling his families."

"He lived in a Chinese restaurant and ended up being jailed in a detention center by mistake."

The boy, whose name Rogers declined to give, was soon released and is now the No 1 student in his class.

Rogers is also active in the local foreign community. He has compiled a city guide with useful tips such as how to find a plumber, where to have a haircut and how to convert money.

In 2007, he was awarded a Lei Feng Medal by Liaoning Province. But the American is concerned that the spirit of Lei Feng has started to wane among China's younger generation.

"That worries me and that is why I am making it a trend among youngsters that Lei Feng is cool and inspiring," he says.

"You can take everything from Lei Feng, but the bottom line is his giving spirit. Now and forever, people need this quality."

注释:

1. Leif Rogers, an American living in Liaoning province, is among the legions of enthusiastic admirers of Lei Feng, one of China's most famous soldiers, renowned not for his battlefield exploits but his humanity.

参考译文:雷夫·罗杰斯是个生活在辽宁的美国人,他是众多雷锋的追随者之一。雷锋是中国最著名的战士,但并非因为他在战场上的英勇,而是由于他的善良行为。

2. Lei Feng(1940—1962)became a New China icon in the 1960s for his charitable deeds and good Samaritan altruism, and his legend grew after his sudden death in an accident.

参考译文:雷锋在 60 年代因为其毫不为己专门为人的行为而成为中国偶像,在他因突然事件去世后更成为传奇人物。

3. Rogers didn't learn much about the model soldier during the ride because of the language barrier but the admiring expression on the driver's face when he referred to Lei Feng

piqued his curiosity, which was already fired up by his journey to China.

参考译文：由于语言障碍，罗杰斯并没有从司机那里了解更多关于这个模范战士的情况，但是司机脸上崇拜激动的表情点燃了他对雷锋的好奇心。

4. "That makes a comparison today as so much is about who you are and how much you are recognized."

参考译文：这与当今状况形成了鲜明对比，现在人们更关心的是你的地位和知名度等。

范文 2

词汇 Vocabulary

gregorian calendar 公历

firecrackers 爆竹

达到高潮 culminate

sumptuous 奢华

parade 游行

knapsack 背包

hitchhike 搭车旅游

端午节 Dragon Boat Festival

清明节 Pure Brightness Day/Tomb Sweeping Day

Foreigner: You've been using the western Gregorian calendar for almost a century now, why do you still celebrate the old Chinese Lunar New year as the most important festival of the year?

Chinese: 你知道，我们庆祝农历新年都几千年了。我想我们的后代还会把这个民间的传统节日继承下去。当然庆祝方式已经有了一些变化，尤其在城里。比如说，我们不再称之为新年，而叫春节。在一些大城市的街上不再舞龙灯了，烟花爆竹也是严格禁放的。

Foreigner: Interestingly enough, this tradition is being kept up in the west. In the Chinatowns of some big cities in the west we still have dragon lantern dances and firecrackers.

Chinese: 在农村和许多城市还有舞龙灯的。许多大城市里禁放烟花爆竹,主要是怕污染环境,引起火灾,也怕伤人。

Foreigner: Understandable. How do you celebrate the festival then?

Chinese: 和过去一样,春节依然是家人团聚的日子。压轴戏是一顿丰盛的年夜饭,挺像你们圣诞节和感恩节的晚餐。我们还保留了端午节和中秋节这两个传统节日,已经作为法定假日。另外还有五一、国庆、清明节和新年为法定假日。

Foreigner: Oh yes, you've been celebrating National Day and May Day. You used to hold parades every year too. How do you celebrate them now?

Chinese: 过去游行是大事,现在主要是放假休息。现在大家有钱了,旅游成了新的时尚,也就成了很多人的度假方式。

Foreigner: That's interesting. And where do people usually go for their trips? Do you travel abroad too?

Chinese: 很多人会出国旅游,主要是东南亚国家和地区,新加坡、马来西亚、泰国,还有香港和澳门。也有一部分去欧洲的。

Foreigner: Actually, traveling needn't be very expensive if you just carry a knapsack on your back and hitchhike some of the way.

Chinese: 由于种种原因,这种旅游方式在中国还没有兴起。不过我相信不久年轻人就会尝试这种方式了。

范文 3

词汇 Vocabulary

belittle 小看;贬低

generosity 慷慨

sumptuous lavish 奢华

pop 不请自到 accidental drop in or walk away

at random 随意

go Dutch 各付其账

doughnut 面包圈

elaborate 精心制作

stewed 炖

tripe 可食用的动物内脏

bacon 熏肉

croissant 牛角面包

appetizing 鲜美可口

Foreigner：That's a wonderful meal. I enjoyed it very much. Thank you again.

Chinese：这不算什么，不过是顿便饭，哪天再请你吃顿像样的。

Foreigner：Now that's something I can never understand. Why do you always belittle your own generosity? You were already kind enough to insist on taking the bill all upon yourself, and now you refer to what I would call, if not sumptuous, but certainly quite a proper meal, just a simple meal.

Chinese：这么说吧。我一直想请你吃一顿饭，可总是没找到时间和机会。今天正好在午餐时间碰上了，我来付账挺自然的。我们只不过是顺便走进一家餐馆罢了。

Foreigner：With us in the west, when some friends happen to have a meal together, it would be natural for each to pay for his or her own share.

Chinese：我们呢，有时也各付各的。

Foreigner：The way we eat makes a difference too. The Chinese meals are always communal. All the dishes are common property and you can dig your chopsticks into any one of them. We always order our own dishes, each eating only what he or she ordered.

Chinese：我们现在吃的习惯也在变，年轻人尤其如此。自助餐越来越受欢迎，个人用盘子自取食物。我们也吃麦当劳。

Foreigner：Personally, I much prefer your fast food. You know, the simple kind, steamed baozi and noodle soup. You used to have them in the street, now they have been chased inside, and though a bit cleaner they are very crowded for space, but the food is very delicious and very cheap too.

Chinese：既然你喜欢吃那些东西，那不知道试没试过北京的风味早餐？一般有豆浆、炸油饼和炸糕。老北京人还喜欢吃一些更讲究的，像炸肝儿什么的。

Foreigner: Stewed tripe doesn't sound too inviting for breakfast. I'd rather stick to my traditional English breakfast of eggs and bacon on toast, but usually I don't have the time and have to be satisfied with a continental breakfast of a cup of coffee and a croissant. Generally speaking, Chinese food is the best in the world. Nothing can beat a Chinese feast, but even a simple meal like the one we just had I found most appetizing.

注释：

这不算什么，不过是顿便饭，哪天再请你吃顿像样的。

参考译文：That's perfectly okay, it's just a simple meal and I will treat you to a proper meal someday.

Why do you always belittle your generosity?

参考译文：明明很慷慨，为什么非要这么低调呢？

我们只不过随便走进一家餐馆罢了。

参考译文：We just popped into a restaurant at random.

The Chinese meals are always communal.

参考译文：在中国，所有的菜都是大家共享的。

范文 4

词汇 Vocabulary

lotus 莲花

brightness Apex 光明顶

Celestial Capital 天都

loom 隐现

pinnacles 高山

Illusionary 虚幻

alternation of seasons 四季变化

riot of colors 色彩缤纷

gurgling merrily 快乐地流淌

blazing red 火红

grotesque rocks and legendary Pines 奇松怪石

frigid 寒带

temperate zone 温带

subtropical 亚热带

tropical 热带

fauna 动物群

flora 植物群

shut out 遮住

mountainside 山腰

dignified and magnificent 威严壮丽

topography terrain 地貌

habitat 栖息地

明天我们去游览黄山，我想先向各位简要介绍一下。黄山位于安徽省南部。它宏伟庄严，风光迷人，是中国著名的风景区。1990 年联合国教科文组织世界遗产委员会宣布黄山为世界自然文化遗产。

黄山是一个奇迹：在 154 平方公里的面积上群峰耸立，许多山峰名如其形。"莲花""光明顶"和"天都"是其中最主要的三个，都高达 1800 米以上。阴天时这些高山隐现在雾霭中，如虚幻一般，天晴时则尽展其威严与壮丽。黄山的颜色和形态随四季的更替而逐渐变化。春天，盛开的鲜花色彩缤纷，点缀着四处的山坡；夏天您可以看到青绿的山峰一座连着一座，泉水在欢乐地流着；秋天把整个黄山装扮成红紫相间的世界，正是枫树火红的季节；冬天则把群山变成一个冰与雾的世界，到处是银枝银石。因此自古以来就一直有很多游客到黄山，探求其神秘，惊叹其美景。人们渐渐总结出黄山四大特征：奇松、怪石、云海和温泉。

由于地貌独特，黄山的气候呈垂直变化，山上的植物也明显呈垂直分布：山顶、山腰和山脚的植物分居寒带、温带和亚热带。黄山共有 1500 种植物，其中树木占了三分之一。因此黄山是从事中国植物研究的重要地方。黄山也是种类繁多的动物群的栖息地。黄山的气候四季宜人。由于云海常常遮住太阳，炎热的天气从来不会太久，这使得黄山成了理想的避暑胜地。

注释：

1. 黄山位于安徽省南部。它宏伟庄严、风光迷人，是中国著名风景区

参考译文：Situated in the south of Anhui Province, the Yellow Mountain is a dignified and magnificent tourist attraction in

China.（tourist attraction 既有风景区,又有迷人的意思,达到简化译文的目的）。

2. 在 154 平方公里的面积上群峰耸立,许多山峰名如其形。

参考译文: Within its 154 square kilometer territory, piles of hills scraping the sky, many of which are embodied by their names.

3. 天阴时这些高山隐现在雾霭中,如虚幻一般,天晴时则尽展其威严壮丽。

参考译文: The hills loom in haze, when it's cloudy, in a illusionary way, while it's clear the magnificence and spectacular view are on full play.

4. 黄山的颜色和形态随季节更替而逐渐变化。

参考译文: The color and appearance of Yellow Mountains change gradually along with seasonal alternation.

5. 春天,盛开的鲜花色彩缤纷,点缀山坡;夏天可以看到青翠的山峰一座连着一座,秋天把整个黄山装扮成红紫相间的世界;冬天,到处是银石银枝。

参考译文: Spring sees flowers in riot of colors, dotting the expanse of slop; you will see hill upon hill of green with streams giggling midst them; Autumn dresses the mountains into a world of purple and blazing red; in winter silver rocks and boughs spreading the whole scene.

6. 由于地貌独特,黄山气候呈垂直变化,山上的植物也明显垂直分布。

参考译文: The climate of the Yellow Mountains changes vertically for its topographic uniqueness, so does the flora.

范文 5

词汇 vocabulary

don 带上 put on

yashmak 面纱

dominos 多米诺

strolling 溜达

camouflage 迷彩服

phrase book 语言小册子

Do you know that in Florida it is illegal to wear swimwear while singing in a public place and in Alabama it's against the law to play dominoes on Sunday? And don't be fooled into thinking that it's just America that has some weird laws. In Italy, it's an offence not to have a smile on your face while in the city of Milan, unless you're visiting someone in hospital or attending a funeral.

Foreign customs and behavior can always seem strange, sometimes frightening even. However, to fully enjoy your holiday and avoid conflict it is important to understand other cultures and respect them. The way we dress is important. Most countries are now used to tourists and it certainly isn't necessary to don a sari in India or a yashmak in Tunisia. But wherever you are, it's better not to offend the locals by strolling through the streets in just a pair of shorts or a bikini, unless it's clearly accepted by everyone. Be aware that sometimes offence can lead to anger, assault and even imprisonment. For example, in Barbados, it's illegal for anyone, including children, to dress in camouflage clothing.

Food is another area that can cause problems. They love eating meat that we consider highly inappropriate. When visiting such a country it is important to remember that you are their guest and should not offend anyone for doing something they regard as perfectly normal. In Singapore, smoking in public buildings, littering, chewing gum on public transport are civic crimes and attract instant fines.

There is difference with gestures and body language. Giving the thumbs up in Saudi Arabia is very much offensive, no matter how pleased you are with someone. Pointing used to be thought of as rude in Britain and many other countries, especially with the index finger. And things can get very confusing if you nod your head at people in Greece, Turkey or Bulgaria, as to some this actually means no. It is illegal to make rude gestures or swear in public in Bahrain, and Kenya, and for doing so you could face severe fine.

Another important tip is to learn some of the local language, even if it's just a few sentences from a phrase book. Showing that you've made some effort can go a long way towards better relations with people overseas. Think how you might react if someone from another country was pointing and shouting at you in a language you didn't understand. Most people, regardless of which country they are from, are normally friendly and welcoming as long as they are given the right signals.

注释:

1. But wherever you are, it's better not to offend the locals by strolling through the streets in just a pair of shorts or a bikini, unless it's clearly accepted by everyone.

参考译文:不管身在何处,最好不要穿短裤和比基尼在街上溜达,这会冒犯当地人,除非这样穿戴明显可被人们接受。

2. Showing that you've made effort can go a long way towards better relations with people overseas.

参考译文:表现出善意的努力,可以帮助你与外国人建立更好的关系。

范文 6

词汇 Vocabulary

体型魁梧 strongly built stature

再现 recapture

斗士 warrior

木筏 raft

酋长 chieftain

群岛 archipelago

原木 log

榕树 banyan

鱼叉 fish spear

美拉尼西亚人(Melanisian)

博兰特·洛耶是里利富岛上的名人,他体形魁梧,是一位对美拉尼西亚人感兴趣的年轻冒险家。当我找到他时,他正忙着写一篇关于他新进行的一次航行的文章。 几个月前,他和朋友打赌说,他要再现一个传说:重建神话中的卡里姆木筏,并驾着它出海航行。

太平洋岛屿上有一个关于卡里姆木筏的传说:一位年轻的卡里姆斗士和附近一个部落酋长的女儿相爱了。他们的恋情遭到反对。于是,年轻的斗士决定建造一个大木筏,并在上面储备足够两人吃的食物,然后驾着木筏和心上人远走高飞。老人们说,这只木筏在启程几天后就在乌韦阿岛附近沉没了,而那对年轻的情侣奇迹般地活了下来,并终于幸福地生活在一起。

在一次围火聊天时,洛耶从老人们那儿听到这个传说。于是他请求罗亚提群岛上的两个居民——威利和诺厄帮他重现这个传说,他要重建传说中的木筏,并驾木筏渡海去乌韦阿岛。

威利负责砍凿造木筏所需的原木,这需要他在森林里搜寻几个小时。最后他选择了印度榕树,用一把大斧子砍了下来。砍下这颗巨大的原木用去了几个小时的时间。之后,威利剥去树皮,将木头晒干。

为了尽可能再现造船的真实过程,洛耶要求威利不能使用火柴或打火机生火。于是威利用一根木棒使劲儿在枯叶的表面摩擦,来生火。经过反复摩擦,直到威利的耐性快要磨光的时候,木头终于生着了火。接着,把原木放在火上烤,这样做的目的是防止木筏因吸水太多而沉没。威利又找来一些藤蔓把原木牢固捆在一起。

出发前一天,威利又为这次冒险准备了生活必需品。他手持一支鱼叉,一动不动地站在岩石上,像动物一样,依靠精确的直觉感知猎物的移动,然后伺机捕猎。利用这种原始的捕鱼方式,威利捕捉到足够的鱼。

注释:

1.年轻的斗士决定建造一个大木筏,并在上面储存足够两人吃的食物,然后驾着木筏和心上人一起远走高飞。

参考译文:The young warrior decided to build a large wood raft, in which enough food will be stored for them and with which he will sail afar with his love.

2. 老人们说，这只木筏在启程几天后就在乌韦阿岛附近沉没了，而那对年轻的情侣奇迹般地活了下来，并终于幸福地生活在一起。

参考译文：According to the aged, the raft sank a couple of days after setting on sail, yet the couple survived miraculously and bathed in a happy life thereafter.

3. 为了尽可能再现造船的真实过程，洛耶要求威利不能使用火柴或打火机生火。

参考译文：To replay the process, Loy required Willy to ignite neither with match nor with a lighter.

第七章　教　育

范文 1

词汇 vocabulary

文化参赞 culture counselor

英国使馆文化处 British council

跨国公司 multinational Corporation（MNC or MNLs）

职业外语水平考试 BULATS

打分 Marking

A. 中国加入世贸之后,掌握一门外语,比如英语,显得越来越重要了,特别是对于年轻人。作为英国文化参赞和以英语为母语者,你有什么建议吗?

B.Well, I think it is hard for me to tell how to improve English teaching in China. And China has already made many improvements in English teaching.

I think it's interesting that many Chinese people seem to achieve very good level of English, despite old-fashioned methodology. They have learnt English for several years, but have no functional command of English. But we have the same problem in UK. The British kids study French at school but often can't actually speak French when they graduate from middle school. We are making big reforms and are achieving somewhat better results now. It takes a long time to develop effective ways of teaching people to speak a foreign language.

A. 由于越来越多的跨国公司在中国设办事处，MBA 也随之成为热门。去贵国商学院求学成为我国学子首选之一。你对此趋势有何看法？

B.Yes. MBA is very hot at the moment. We certainly notice that many Chinese students want to do MBAs in the UK. What I would say about MBA is that I think some students in China want to do MBA too early. My personal opinion is that an MBA program is more suitable for people with some work experience, for example, three to four years. And many MBA program in the UK will only accept students that have some work experience. I think that it's quite difficult for students who have never worked in any kind of business or public organization to understand the meaning of management theory content. So, I wonder whether it is a good idea for so many young Chinese students wanting to study in UK?

A. 贵文化处向那些想留学英国的中国学生提供什么帮助呢？

B.Well, we are happy to advice Chinese students. We get very large number of Chinese students going to UK every year and the number is increasing very quickly. This year I estimate that about 16,000 new students will go to the UK. That is an increase of 1/3 on last year's number. Many of these students will go for several years in the United Kingdom. They enter British universities to take an undergraduate degree. Some remain to do a master's degree.

We welcome the students, but also, we hope that they will choose the program carefully to meet their personal needs. They are always welcome to talk to my staff in British Council in China. We can give them free advice to help them decide what they want to do. In many ways we are trying to help these self-financed students to make good choice.

A. 据说英国学费和生活费很高,你怎么看?

B.I think the main attraction of studying in UK is the quality and variety of education. But we think sometimes people exaggerate the price. However, I've also emphasized that we don't expect to rely on low prices to attract more students from China. Choosing your study abroad is a very big decision. It costs you a lot of money and a lot of time and it may determine your future life. For most people, it's a turning point. Probably it's one of the two big decisions you make in your life, the other one might be getting married. Usually, people don't marry someone they met yesterday. So, it's generally not a good idea to make a study abroad decision in one day either.

A. 英国文化处在中国举行许多考试,如雅思、职业外语水平考试等。鉴于雅思在想去英国留学学生中最流行,你能简要介绍一下这个考试吗?

B.Yes. We are directly involved in IELS and BULATS. IELS is very hot at the moment. Now the British Universities are attracting large number of Chinese applicants. I think they mostly tend to insist on good IELS scores. But the test is also very widely used by students going to study in Australia, New Zealand and Canada, even in the USA. Maybe most people in China don't know that the majority of American universities accept the IELS scores.

A. 从贵处考试结果看,你认为中国学生最常见的弱项是什么?

B. It is quite common to find candidates' writing skills are quite weak and less developed than other skills. It's also quite common to find candidates whose reading is good but too slow, and that will affect their marks in the reading test. I think when the Chinese students study English, they spend a lot of time doing intensive reading, but reading speed is sometimes a problem. These are important skills if you are going to studying in the UK. You need to have good writing skills to pass the course and you need to read quickly to keep up.

A. 你们今年对雅思有什么改进？

B. To ensure the security of the test we will make improvements to it each year. And this year there will be more standardization of the speaking test to make the marking reliable. The speaking test is carried out by our trained interviewers. They must be native speakers; they must have ELTT or applied linguistics qualification at postgraduate level and English teaching experience. Those are the basic qualifications for examiners of the writing and speaking test. They also have to be certified as IELS examiners after carrying out some trial marking and receiving training. For the writing and speaking test, the marking has to be made by qualified examiners to ensure that the marking is reliable and test takers get the right mark in IELS test.

范文 2

词汇 vocabulary

融入 merge

inclusive 包涵；包容

tolerant 宽容

beat around the bush 拐弯抹角

华裔 ethnic Chinese

feel quite a tease 感觉好玩好笑

Journalist: 作为华裔，您认为当市长和身为澳籍华人两种身份有无冲突？

Mr. Yan: I don't believe it's a conflict. Australia is a multicultural society and it's a country of migrants. Immigrants settle in Australia from different countries and regions with different backgrounds, culture and history. When someone decides to settle in Australia, he or she becomes an Australian, so I'm a Chinese-Australian. I feel quite a tease with my two capacities.

Journalist：我们的读者都在学英语，他们很想达到用英文思维的水平，无需先做汉译英。您是怎样实现这一点的？

Mr. Yan：One way of achieving that is to live in a country where English is the native language. If you can use it as much as possible everyday, that is to say, you hear it, you speak it and read it then gradually you'll achieve it. When I first went to Australia, language was a problem. Like all the Chinese students, I had to translate Chinese into English in my mind. After many years of hard efforts, I completed the thinking process in English before speaking. I no longer need to do that. I believe over years of practice; you'll get used to it.

Journalist：您的专业是工商管理，并曾做过高层经理人，您事业的转折点是什么？

Mr. Yan：It depends on what you want to achieve in your life. Money is important but it's not everything. Money, I believe is means of achieving an end. It's not an objective because you can't take money with you when you go. We live a life that we think we are happy not just because we have money. A lot of rich people are not happy. Life is what you make all of it. I'm very happy though I'm not rich. As a mayor I'm happy and when retired not being a mayor I'll still be happy. I believe I'm making a contribution to the society and I'm achieving something is worthwhile to achieve. Comparing with making money, making a positive contribution to the society is more important. We should not just think about ourselves because there are always a lot of others less fortunate than ourselves. We'll see what we can do for them not just for ourselves.

Journalist：您此次来华的目的是什么，您想通过这次访问做点什么？

Mr. Yan：What I've been trying to do is to improve the relationship and to promote better cooperation and exchange between people of Adelaide and other Chinese cities. I believe there are a lot of things we can work together. And China is providing a lot of opportunities for the rest of the world and for me, an ethnic Chinese I'm proud of what is happening in China. I'd like to be part of it. At the same time, I'm proud of the city I represent because it's an attractive, beautiful and friendly city. I'd like to see more Chinese go to my city to visit, to study and even to settle there. We need more people and I believe the city of Adelaide will benefit from more migrants and students form China.

Journalist: 您在澳大利亚居住了 30 多年,您能据您的经验就如何融入主流社会给初到异国的人一些建议吗?

Mr. Yan: Well, if you are a new arrival as a foreigner in Australia, obviously you want to live and work together with people that you share the same language and culture with. But gradually you'll start mixing with people from other backgrounds and if you want to be successful in your business or career, you must get involved in the mainstream community. How? To be part of it and you got to make the first step yourself. I had seen people who live in Sydney for a life and had never gone out of the China town. Usually, they are the people who have language problems. He can't mix with Australians for he can't communicate with them. So, communication is required first.

And then you also have to be willing to go and mix. Because Chinese is a minority in Australia, if you want to be successful there you have to be in the mainstream. That depends on the individual. Nobody is going to force you to do one thing or another. If you are not willing, it's up to you.

Journalist: 您怎么评价澳大利亚人?

Mr. Yan: They are very easy-going people in general. The country is a large country with a lot of open space so Australian people like outdoor activities very much and are inclusive and tolerant towards others. Australians are usually very straightforward, for example, if they don't like something, they will say it and won't beat around the bush.

Journalist: 在我看来,您很成功,您有没有受过挫折?

Mr. Yan: I've done through many defeats. For instance, the first time I attempted to become the Lord Mayor was a defeat. I lost the election but I decided that I'd try again and eventually I succeeded. Life is not always roses but the attitude is very important. I believe a positive attitude towards life is critical for the positive outcome. I see experience as a learning process and there is more than one way to achieve the objective. A lot of people think their way is the only way. They need to be more tolerant and inclusive.

注释:

Life is what you make all of it.

参考译文:是你赋予了生活意义。

范文 3

词汇 Vocabulary

open up 开始发展;展示

prestigious 著名;有声望的

bearing 关系;影响

fare 进展;成功

hit and miss 时而成功时而不成功

ins and outs 复杂详情

cram 死记硬背

spit 突出;说出

rehash 重复(争论)

come out on top 出人头地

idiosyncrasy 气质性;嗜好

slate 选定

count on 指望

shot 机会

For most of us, success in school has very little to do with actual learning. The most important thing you have to master is how to play the grade game. Once you devise your own strategies for getting high marks, everything opens up to you. You may be admitted to a prestigious college or win a scholarship, not to mention gaining the admiration of your teachers and parents.

When you are taking a test and you know that your grade depends on the result of that examination, any interest you might have had in the subject's content becomes secondary to trying to read the teacher's mind in attempting to supply the answer he wants. Whatever you've learned about the subject becomes of little consequence if it isn't what's asked for on the test. The test grade to a large extent supposedly reflects your subject knowledge; it may have a tremendous bearing on how you fare in the course. And, therefore, it becomes more important than anything else you might have gotten out of the class.

Not everyone does well on tests. At times, it can almost run into a ridiculous game of hit and miss. Some kids haven't mastered the art of test taking, some panic under pressure or need more time or another way to express what they know.

Being an academic success means learning the ins and outs of the school system. Then you have to work things to your advantage. A lot of kids are already doing it without even realizing it.

Take selecting courses for example. Before scheduling your classes, it's essential to learn as much as you can about who's teaching what from the older kids. You have to find out who's an easy grader as well as who's really tough. Some teachers give tests taken directly from the class notes. It's important to know this because if you have cram for another exam, you can skip reading the book in this case. Most of the teachers only require that you're good at memorizing and are able to mindlessly spit back what was said in class.

It's just about guaranteed that these teachers will give you an A if you do the work. You just rehash the class periods on your test papers. A few of the teachers require a little more thinking in your answers. Although their classes may seem more challenging and thought-provoking, you can never be sure what unusual questions will turn up on their tests. If there's a chance of doing poorly in a subject they've studied for, most kids will try to avoid these teachers. The pressure on us to come out on top is so great that we can't afford to take risks.

Getting high grades also depends on becoming aware of each teacher's little idiosyncrasies. For example, everyone in school knows that Mrs. Philip, who teaches ninth grade English, is crazed when it comes to neatness. At times she doesn't even seem rational about it. It's almost as if to her a tidy but poorly thought-out paper is worth more than one which is on target and well written but isn't as neat.

Once I'd selected the teacher whom I'd wanted for chemistry only to find that my guidance counselor had me slated for another period. Science has always been difficult for me. With a tough teacher I'd be likely to pull a lower B in this course and my class rank would probably go down. I'm among the top twenty kids now, and I need to at least break into the top ten in order to get into a big-name college.

I had to take chemistry, so one day in between classes I talked to the teacher I had originally wanted. I told him how I'd heard what a really good teacher he was, and how disappointed I was that I'd have to graduate without having been in his class. I lied. It worked. I had counted on the chemistry teacher being human, and he was. I wasn't proud of myself for what I did. But I considered it part of the grade game we are pushed into playing to even get a shot at going to the best schools.

A lot of that kind of thing goes on at school on almost every level. When you apply to most colleges, you need to supply reference letters from your teachers. The fonder they are of you, the better the picture they are likely to paint. Besides, when a teacher is not sure whether to give a student an A-minus, or a

B-plus, his personal impression of the kid has somehow got to be taken into account.

The result of all this is that the Spanish kids take Spanish and the Chinese kids take Chinese, although they already know these languages. They might profit more from learning a new language, but usually they feel forced to take the easy way out. It's all got to do with the pressure for grades. The drive to learn something new and worthwhile, or even to try something that looks interesting but that you're not quite sure you'd be able to master, has to be channeled elsewhere. Most parents seem to feel that going to school is the only thing a kid has to do, and you're expected to do it well.

When I tell this to people outside the school scene, often they'll ask me what all this has to do with learning. I have to admit – not much. In school the pressure for grades far outweighs the joy and interest you might experience in learning something new. While you are in a classroom setting, actual understanding is not as important as making teacher think that you have a grasp of the material. I'm little more than a young runner in the junior rat race. My dad works in an advertising firm, and he's always saying that he has to give his clients what they want. He says that he has to understand their expectations in order to come up with a working formula.

Students do much of the same thing. We have to come up with the right answers. And although in real life there may be more than one acceptable solution, most teachers do not afford us that kind of leeway in class. Generally, there's only one right answer. Any other way of tackling a problem becomes, at best, less right.

A school you exchange the right answers for high grade, and at graduation you trade in your class credits for the badge or diploma. Then you try to get into the best college possible. And the whole thing starts all over. You become so interested in achieving that it's hard to examine if you've actually learned anything meaningful along the way.

注释:

1. Once you devise your own strategies for getting high marks, everything opens up to you.

参考译文:一旦有了自己得高分的策略,一切都会顺风顺水。

2. When you are taking a test and you know that your grade depends on the result of that examination, any interest you might have had in the subject's content becomes secondary to trying to read the teacher's mind in attempting to supply the answer he wants.

参考译文:考试时,你很清楚分数取决于考试结果,这时对该科目有无兴趣已经不是最重要的了,重要的是知道老师想要什么,并据此给出他想要的答案。

3. The drive to learn something new and worthwhile, or even to try something that looks interesting but that you are not quite sure you'd be able to master, has to be channeled elsewhere.

参考译文:学新东西,有价值的东西的冲动,甚至只是尝试那些看上去挺有意思的内容的想法都不得不做出让步,因为你没有把握自己可以掌握它。

4. I'm a little more than a young runner in the junior rat race.

参考译文:我只是个菜鸟。

5. Any other way of tackling a problem becomes, at best, less right.

参考译文:其他任何作答,都不是百分百正确。

范文 4

词汇 Vocabulary

context 上下文;背景

ardor 热情

carry on 继续

persecute 迫害

incredulously 怀疑

incur 招致

antagonism 对抗 敌意

precede 先于

trait 特征

"Let the world know China and let China know the world". I can't remember exactly where I saw this slogan in Beijing and what the context was. Given the simple fact of the ardor people have for learning foreign languages and the number of people going abroad each year, everyone can tell how hard China and the Chinese people are trying to know the world. But I didn't know how equally important and urgent it is for the world to know China until I came to the States.

First let me give you an idea of how little China is known to the Americans by quoting some of the questions I was asked by the graduate students at the department of communication at Purdue University.

"Where is Beijing? Is it a coastal city?" "Why do you carry on the one-child family policy? Don't you know it is a crime?"

"I hope you don't mind my asking this question. Do Chinese people still live in poverty and oppression?"

"Is it true that anyone who practices religion will be persecuted in China?"

The list of surprises I was given by my fellow American graduate students can go on and on, but let me in turn give you some examples of the surprises we gave to them.

In the self-introduction during our first class in a Ph. D course, when I told them I wanted to finish my studies for the degree as soon as I could and then go back to China, the American students looked at me in both surprise and disbelief. Their assumption is that everybody, including Chinese of course, who comes to the States will stay here to seek a better life and that this is the only place where one can find a better life.

When I asked my officemate for advice about buying a new car, she stared at me, asking me incredulously: "A new car?" later I found out that her surprise was due to the popular image of Chinese students: either too poor or too economical.

When American TA asked me what I told my undergraduate students about my feelings on the September 11 Attack, I repeated my answer: "I'm sad and angry. I'm sad because I know what it feels like to lose somebody you love. I have lost my father-in-law. I'm angry because I know what it feels like when one's motherland is attacked. Our Chinese embassy in Yugoslavia was bombed in 1999 by NATO. That was an attack no different from one against my motherland." She shook her head in shock and disbelief. I knew what she was thinking: how dare you, a Chinese TA, voice such strong opinions, especially one which might incur antagonism among your American students? She is just like other Americans who are so used to Chinese students being silent or reserved.

When we Chinese students for the first time joined the monthly performance hour of the department and sang some traditional songs and preceded each song with a brief humorous introduction, all the faculty and students present were astonished. To them, Chinese students are so serious, shy or even withdrawn. These traits have been partly responsible for the consequence that Chinese students are sometimes invisible.

I'm aware that I can't simply use these examples from my own experience to argue for the ignorance of China among the Americans and their bias against the Chinese people. But if you consider the fact that they are either PhD or MA students of communication, how can you be more optimistic about the general Americans' understanding of China and their image of the Chinese people.

注释：

1. But I didn't know how equally important and urgent it is for the worried to know China until I came to the States.

参考译文：直到来美国后我才知道让世界了解中国同样急迫和重要。

2. First let me give you an idea of how little China is known to the Americans by quoting some of the questions I was asked by the graduate students at the department of communication at Purdue University.

参考译文：首先我要通过普渡大学交流专业研究生对我的提问来展示一下美国人对中国的了解是多么有限。

3. The list of surprises I was given by my fellow American graduate students can go on and on, but let me in turn give you some examples of the surprises we gave to them.

参考译文：那些美国研究生同学让我惊讶的事情数不胜数，但我想反过来说一下我们让他们感到惊讶的事情。

4. How dare you, a Chinese TA, voice such strong opinions, especially one which might incur antagonism among your American students?

参考译文：你一个中国助教怎么敢说出这么强悍的观点，特别是它可能会引发美国学生的敌意？

第八章 经 济

范文 1

词汇 Vocabulary

gadgets 小工具；小配件

instrumental 重要作用

infomercial 专题广告

documercial 文献类广告

netherworld 冥界

dehydrator 脱水机

citrus 柑橘类水果

regimen 养生之道

endorsement 给……背书

genesis 开始 起源

hold... accountable for 让……为……负责

opine 表示意见

metamorphosis 涅槃；质变

In 1964 a gadget inventor and salesman named Ron Popeil started a company named Ronco and became instrumental in creating the television infomercial industry in the U.S.

Poised between superficial talk shows and the strident tones of Madison Avenue. The half-hour ads originally existed in a kind of television netherworld – shown only late at nigh after most consumers had gone to bed. By 1995, however, infomercials were no longer limited to appliances such as Ronco food dehydrator. Their products ranged from high-priced Barbie dolls to citrus fruit, from skin –and-hair-care products to diet regimens, and from investment advice to methods for improving interpersonal relationships.

Modern infomercials usually relied on celebrity endorsem- ents rather than high-pressure salesmen to lend credibility to their products. Singers Dionne Warwick had been affiliated with the Psychic Friends Network for almost a decade, while actresses Meredith Baxter and Ali McGraw both appeared in popular infomercials for Victoria Jackson Cosmetics. Covert Bailey, a familiar face on public television, advertised an exercise machine, and veteran actress Angela Lansbury brought children's literature to infomercials by promoting a series of Beatrix Potter stories on videotape.

Infomercials also showed they had great potential for profit. The National Infomercial Marketing Association International (NIMA), the trade association for the industry, estimated that in 1994 the ads brought in $1 billion in product sales. NIMA played an important role in reinforcing marketing guidelines and in holding the companies accountable for the claims they made for their products. NIMA also presented yearly awards for excellence within the industry. In 1995 fitness expert Jake Steinfeld swept the field, winning infomercial of the year, best product, and best product offer.

More recently, program-length commercial gained in popularity among mainstream products. Many companies opined that a standard 60-second television commercial was not long enough to present their products thoroughly, so they began turning to an offspring of infomercials called documercials to fill the need for more in-depth advertising. Documercials generally concentrated on promoting a product or company image rather than on direct sales. Familiar names included the Toyota and Ford motor companies, Sears, Roebuck and Co., American Airlines, and Eastman Kodak. In a bid for a younger audience, Sega of America released an infomercial describing new software for its Genesis video game machine, running the ad for four weeks during the 1994 holiday season.

Industry executives predicted a metamorphosis of the infomercial, which would be crucial to its survival in the second half of the decade. There was an effort to make infomercials more sophisticated by making various technical improvements. Some political candidates had begun to use documercial-like programs to promote themselves and their policies. The ads had even found their way onto the internet. Direct-response marketers often made the claim that infomercials were the first interactive medium, and their appearance on the information superhighway seemed to many to be a natural step in their evolution.

注释：

1. In 1964 a gadget inventor and salesman named Ron Popeil started a company named Ronco and became instrumental in creating the television infomercial industry in the U.S.

参考译文：1964 年，小工具发明人和销售员罗柏培创立了洛克公司，同时他对美国电视专题广告产业的兴起发挥了重要作用。

2. Poised between superficial talk shows and the strident tones of Madison Avenue, the half-hour ads originally existed in a kind of television netherworld – shown only late at nigh after most consumers had gone to bed.

参考译文：作为兼有肤浅脱口秀和麦迪逊大街式刺耳叫卖特点的一档节目，这种 30 分钟广告节目起初只在午夜播出，此时大多数消费者都已入睡。

3. Modern infomercials usually relied on celebrity endorsements rather than high-pressure salesmen to lend credibility to their products.

参考译文：现在的专题广告依靠名人带货而不是靠压力极大的销售员来卖力推销。

范文 2

词汇 Vocabulary

mayhem 混乱

year-on-year 同比

month-on-month 环比

ambit 周围

real estate 房地产

slew 回转

realty 不动产

sizzling 热烈地

price hikes 价格巅峰

iron out 消除

hub 中心 枢纽

After the mayhem, order seems to be returning to the nation's property market as the monthly price growth rate slowed in March, an indication that the government's tightening measures are finally bearing fruit.

Property prices in 70 of China's large and medium-sized cities rose 11.7 percent year-on-year in March, the National Bureau of Statistics (NBS) said on Wednesday.

That topped the 10.7 percent increase recorded in February and the 9.5 percent in January. It was also the biggest year-on-year increase for a single month after the NBS expanded its coverage ambit to 70 cities in July.

However, in sharp contrast, the month-on-month growth rate, a key indicator of the short-term trend, slowed by 0.2 percentage points in March.

The NBS does not release monthly growth rate figures, but

industry circles said the price growth rates are calculated based on the differences between the growth rates of the first three months.

"The sharp increase in March was partly due to the low base of last year when the overall market remained weak due to the global recession. The lower month-on-month growth rate, however, means that the government policies are slowly making an impact," said Danny Ma, senior director of CBRE Research China, a real estate researcher.

The government launched a slew of measures late last year to curb excessive property price growth in some cities. These measures included rules on taxation, credit and land supply.

"The growth rate is sliding, but prices may continue to rise until the demand supply imbalance improves," said Ma.

Developers had deferred construction of new projects till the fourth quarter of last year due to the global financial crisis. But with the recovery beginning to take shape and the realty market sizzling, it led to a demand-supply imbalance and resulted in sharp price hikes.

Qin, a senior researcher with the Ministry of Housing and Urban-Rural Development, said the imbalances would be ironed out soon.

Joan Wang, associate director of Research & Consultancy at Savills Beijing feels that April would be a better determinant of the realty trend due to seasonal factors. Given the Spring Festival in February and annual sessions of China's top legislature political advisory body in March, property transactions during these two months are normally low.

According to the NBS data, Haikou, the capital city of Hainan, showed the biggest gain last month, with a 53.9 percent jump in property prices, Sanya, also in Hainan, was the next with a 52.1 percent increase. Property prices rose sharply following the government's plan to reshape the island as an international tourist hub.

Property sales during the first three months of the year surged 57.7 percent to 797.7 billion yuan from the same period last year. Investment in real estate development rose 35.1 percent to 659.4 billion yuan over the same period, NBS said.

注释：

1. After a mayhem order seems to be returning to the nation's property market as the monthly price growth rate slowed in March, an indication that the government's tightening measures are finally bearing fruit.

参考译文：在一番混乱之后，国家的房地产市场似乎回归正常，当月价格增长率在三月放缓，这说明政府的紧缩措施终于有了结果。

2. That topped the 10.7 percent increase recorded in February and the 9.5 percent in January. It was also the biggest year-on-year increase for a single month after the NBS expanded its coverage ambit to 70 cities in July.

参考译文：这也超过了一月份10.7%和二月份9.5%的增长。这也是当月最大的同比增长，此前，统计局将其监测范围扩大到七十个城市。

3. "The sharp increase in March was partly due to the low base of last year when the overall market remained weak due to the global recession."

参考译文：三月份急剧的增长部分原因是去年的低起点，当时总体市场因全球的衰退而表现疲软。

4. Price rose sharply following the government's plan to reshape the island as in international tourist hub.

参考译文：在政府计划将这个海岛打造成为国际旅游枢纽之后，房价急剧上升。

范文 3

词汇 Vocabulary

BS：理学学士

setback 挫折

ingredients 成分，要素

differentiate 使……不同

consolidation 合并

robust 活力

delve 钻研

vallum 堡垒

viability 可行性

Reporter：据我所知，您于 1956 年毕业于耶鲁大学，获理学学士学位，并于 1962 年毕业于哈佛大学，获工商管理硕士。此后投身商界，升迁迅速。能透露一下成功秘诀吗？

Mr. Chairman：Oh, my key to success is to surround yourself with good people and to listen to them. And the two universities are both very important to me.

Reporter：朗讯作为全球最大的网络通信器材供应商，它一直都很成功。你们的制胜之道是什么？对于目前的挫折，你们将采取什么对策？

Chairman：I think the key to success is the combination of world leading technology and world leading human talents. In my experience it has always been the two most important ingredients. In order to serve the customer better, you have to have technologies differentiating you from others and you have to have human talents that can understand the technology and try to bring it to bear the customers in a way that is truly helpful.

I think right now the industry is going through a period of consolidation. We had very robust demand from 1998 to 2000 and the demand now is very much reduced and the key here is to delve very strong vallums of the one thing whether the stock will continue to invest in technology in a way that increases the leadership position that we now enjoy.

Reporter：1995 年你曾任朗讯的董事长和首席执行官，而今你再次担任董事长。在您的两个任期中，发展战略有什么变化吗？

Chairman：No. I think the company has always been trying to position itself to be the major provider of technology, software and hardware for service providers and by concentrating totally on that market, we believe that technology will increasingly differentiate our customers. And yes, I think we've been successful and I think we'll remain successful as the largest provider of technology to service providers of the world and that allows us to make the most investment in technologies which in turn help our customers, we believe at the leadership position.

Reporter：您在中国有几千员工。作为朗讯董事长，你认为他们的长处和短处各是什么？

Chairman：Yes, many thousands. We find China to be full of talented people. It is the largest market we have outside the United States and we have several-thousand people here dedicated to serving the Chinese service providers in a way that will differentiate their offerings. We have the labs here and we have service and innovation centers here and we are increasing roughly 50 percent a year over the last two years, so it has been a very tremendous market and the market we intend to serve as a leader in long term.

Reporter：朗讯在华投资有 35 亿美元，而且在世界其他地方也设了办事处。据此，你能谈一下全球化吗？

Chairman：Yes, I think globalization is a healthy phenomenon because it brings people from different countries together and it reduces space and time that tend to confuse people of different cultures and different backgrounds. And I think one advantage of globalization is it brings the best of thinking from China, together with other parts of the world and therefore encourages an increase in the standard of living around the world. I think it is a very good thing though obviously there are issues that need to be deal with to make sure the standard of living increases for all people. And that is part of the challenge for all of us.

Reporter：我记得在你的一次讲话中说，拉索女士（现任首席执行官）重返朗讯，将带来出色的销售业绩和良好的客户关系技能。你是指女性更善于销售及处理客户关系吗？

Chairman：Oh, I think that one has to think about the best talent available irrespective of the person's color and irrespective of the person's gender or the person's nationality. So, I think corporations around the world that avail themselves all of the skills available will always do better than people that do not. I don't think it has anything to do with gender, I think it has to do with competence.

Reporter：一个小问题，董事长和首席执行官的职能有何不同？

Chairman：Well, it depends on how a corporation is set up, but the CEO is the major executive of the corporation and as my role the chairman is to first chair the board of directors and to help in any way I can to ensure that the company is meeting the needs of its customers. The president is in charge of all the day-to-day operations of the company.

Reporter：朗讯作为通信业巨头为何还要改组及重新定位？

Chairman：Yes. The major issue that the company is facing and all other companies in this field are facing is that the very large demand that drove the operations from 1995 – 2000 has diminished rapidly and therefore companies need to reposition themselves in a way that they can successfully continue to invest in technologies and meet the needs of service providers in the long term. So, all equipment producers are going through a period of restructuring, moving from a very high level of demand to a demand at a much lower level and the company has done that very successfully and I think Lucent has led the way and will be the major supplier over an extended period of time.

注释:

1. 此后投身商界,升迁迅速。能透露一下成功秘诀吗?

参考译文:You engaged in the business world afterwards, and get quick promotion. Can you disclose the secret of success?

2. In order to serve the customer better, you have to have technologies differentiating you from others and you have to have human talents that can understand the technology and try to bring it to bear the customers in a way that is truly helpful.

参考译文:为更好地服务顾客,最好拥有能使你有别他人的技术,同时有能解读这些技术,并能够用该技术服务于顾客的人才,这一点非常重要。

3. 1995 年你曾任朗讯的董事长和首席执行官,而今你再次担任董事长。在您的两个任期中,发展战略有什么变化吗?

参考译文:You worked as the chairman and CEO of Lucent in 1995, and now you come back to pick up the same job. Is there any strategic change between your two terms?

4. And yes, I think we've been successful and I think we'll remain successful as the largest provider of technology to service providers of the world and that allows us to make the most investment in technologies which in turn help our customers, we believe at the leadership position.

参考译文:的确,我觉得我们一直很成功,我们还将继续成功的作为服务器提供商背后的最大的技术供应商。这样我们就能够在技术上做最大的投资,反之这种投资会帮助我们的客户在他们的领域始终处于领导地位。

范文 4

词汇 Vocabulary

shed(股份)下跌

bondholder 债券持有人

IOU 欠条

evaporate 消失;蒸发

crater 失败

demise 死掉;毁掉

rampant 蔓延；猖獗的 flourishing excessively, unrestrained

file for 提出申请；诉讼

boom 繁荣发展 quick development

downturn 下跌 recession in economy

resilience 恢复 recovery in dynamics or spirit

novel 新颖 new and strange

shakeout 重组 restructure, reform

stake 赌注 share in business speculation

stagnation 僵化；停滞 dull and unsuccessful

mount 增加 increase in quantity

audit 审计 check account

vouch 承诺担保 guarantee

corporate 法人的

当电信巨人世界通信公司寻求破产保护之后，痛苦便开始四处蔓延。道琼斯平均工业指数又一次下跌235点。世通债券的持有人发现手中价值几十亿的票据转眼就变成了分文不值的欠条。世通的生意伙伴开始担忧是否还能收回成本。世界通信公司价值1070亿美元的资产前途未卜。

这是自世界通信公司透露隐瞒近40亿美元费用后，几周以来各方所遭受的苦难之后的又一次重击。价值1000多亿的公司股票顷刻化为乌有，数千员工被裁失业，股民信心一落千丈。

然而在这满天乌云之中，世界通信公司的破产也显示出美国经济健康的一面。

破产对于经济长期健康的发展是很重要的。即便在繁荣的时期，美国公司的破产也是层出不穷。实际上，在上一个经济繁荣期，申请破产保护的公司总数要比最近萧条期的总数要大。

美国经济体系的韧性或自我修复能力，便是建立在这种"创造性破坏"的基础之上。经营有方的公司取代了经营不善的公司；新产品、新服务替代过时的产品和服务；投资流向盈利最高的企业。

在电信业，这一过程表明，20世纪90年代后期巨大的超额投资，需要用正在进行的艰难的重组来调整。这种调整是痛苦的，但是如果不这样，其结果会更糟。日本保护其大公司免遭破产，努力保住了工人的饭碗,投资者的股份,还有经理们的荣誉,但结果是十年的经济停滞。

创造性破坏要求向投资者和员工就一个公司越来越严重的问题进行通报,而这正是世界通信公司以及众多其他公司所力图掩盖的。保证公司遵循最严格的道德规范就需要进行重大改革。这些改革包括禁止会计师事务所向其审计的公司销售其他服务,严格执行财会制度,要求首席执行官为其公司财务报表进行个人担保,严惩法人犯罪等。

注释:

1. 当电信巨人世界通信公司寻求破产保护之后,痛苦便开始四处漫。

参考译文: After the telecom giant WorldCom sought Chapter 11 protection, pain began to radiate in all directions. (Chapter 11: 美国破产法第十一章为破产保护,现已成为表达法)。

2. 道琼斯平均工业指数又一次下跌 235 点。

参考译文: The Dow Jones industrial average shed another 235 points.

3. 世界通信公司价值 1070 亿美元的资产前途未卜。

参考译文: WorldCom's $107 billion in assets faced an uncertain fate.

4. 这是自世界通信公司透露隐瞒近四十亿美元费用后,几周以来各方所遭受的苦难之后的又一次重击。

参考译文: This is on top of the suffering already underway in the weeks since WorldCom disclosed it hid nearly $4 billion in costs.

5. 然而在这满天乌云之中,世界通信公司的破产也显示出美国经济健康的一面。

参考译文: Yet amid all the gloom, WorldCom's demise points to something healthy about the U.S. economy. (为避免重复,这里用 demise 表示破产)。

6. 美国经济体制的韧性和自我修复能力,便是建立在这种"创造性破坏"之上。

参考译文: The resilience of American economic system is based on letting this "creative destruction "take place.

7. 创造性破坏要求向投资者和员工就一个公司越来越严重的问题进行通报,而这正是世界通信公司和众多其他公司所力图掩盖的。

参考译文: Creative destruction requires fair notice to investors and workers of a company's mounting problems, something WorldCom and far too many other companies tried to hide.

第九章 科 技

范文 1
词汇 Vocabulary
premise 前提
unprejudiced 无偏见
paradigm 范式
galaxy 星系
immunology 免疫学
molecule 分子
antibody 抗体
receptor 受体
sequence 制订……序列
code 指定遗传密码
vaccine 疫苗
therapeutic 治疗的
exhilaration 狂喜
complexity 复杂性
elude 无法得到,使记不得
gratification 满足

unattainable 无法获得的

incapacitate 使残疾

dyslexia 诵读困难

deficiency 缺陷

Fundamental Science has provided us with an increasingly detailed and accurate understanding of nature and the world around us. Progress in Science is based on the premises that:

Everything, including existing knowledge, is open to critical, unprejudiced inquiry. Science is often built on the destruction of existing paradigms and is a continuously evolving process.

Our minds, reason, and our powers of observation are the tools we used to advance knowledge. There are no mysteries that will resist scientific investigation.

Science is the property of mankind and not of any one nation or people and is our most precious human asset.

Scientists have been extremely successful in the last century in all fields, physics, chemistry, biology, and genetics. Their discoveries have had a dramatic impact on medicine and our life pattern. We are gaining the power but not necessarily always the wisdom to control our lives, our environment, our fate on this earth and galaxy.

In my own field, immunology, a division of biomedical science, it has been my privilege to witness in the last 40 years spectacular advances. The cells of the immune system have been identified, the specific molecules they produce, have been purified and sequenced and the genes that code for them have been cloned.

Such basic knowledge is being translated into increasing benefits to health through applied technology and should soon contribute to vaccine development against AIDS and cancer. Enormous advances have similarly been made in other areas of biomedical science, with discovery of the structure of nucleic acids, the genetic code, the control of growth and differentiation at the cellular level, which should soon permit the development of new generations of therapeutic drugs against cancer.

Of my own work in the lab over the last 45 years, I would like to share with you two of the most exciting aspects which are very well worth the years of efforts and the difficulties encountered. These are:

The exhilarating feeling that one experiences when Nature, for the first time, reveals its closely guarded secrets, and one begins to finally understand some of the complexities that have eluded us for many years.

The warm and intimate intellectual relationships that are established between teacher and student in the lab in the course of conducting research together, which constitute the training process. I have had the pleasure and personal gratification of training in my lab more than 80 younger scientists. Many of whom have made very successful careers, and made important contributions themselves. Several of my students have been of Chinese descent.

What about the future? I'm convinced that the future will be even more exciting than the past. As I told my grandson, I very much envy him and I would like to be his age and have the opportunity to become again a scientist, starting in another field, and to have a chance to push further the frontiers of knowledge. I urge many of you, who read these lines, to do the same. Science is a very exciting experience as well as a worthwhile life goal, because only those undertakings that challenge us to develop our minds and energies to attempt the unattainable are worthy of us.

If I had been given the chance to live another life as a scientist in the 21 centuries, I would study the brain and investigate the mechanism of consciousness, reasoning, logic, and memory, and I would try to understand how this marvelous machine, that evolution has developed, is capable of analyzing itself and of understanding the world and reality. This is the ultimate challenge, which I dare you to devote your life to, and to solve for the glory and benefit of mankind.

The most precious message I want to convey to the young is that your lives offer you an opportunity to leave a mark in history for the benefit of mankind. No project should be impossible to accomplish if one is properly determined to succeed and not to spare one's energy and resources.

To those who were born with an incapacitating condition, the example of my life and success should bring hope and courage. I was born severely dyslexia. I had difficulty learning how to read and could never spell correctly in any of the languages I have learned. I was rescued by the PC and the word processor which corrects my mistakes. I want you to realize that a deficiency such as dyslexia was for me, should be considered a challenge to conquer rather than a shortcoming to be sorry for.

注释：

1. The cells of the immune system have been identified, the specific molecules they produce, have been purified and sequenced and the genes that code for them have been cloned.

参考译文：免疫系统的细胞已经被识别，它们产生的分子已经净化并进行顺序排列，为它们编码的基因已经被克隆。

2. The exhilarating feeling that one experiences when nature, for the first time, reveals its closely guarded secrets, and one begins to finally understand some of the complexities that have eluded us for many years.

参考译文：当大自然第一次显露它曾经紧密防护的秘密，当你可以最终明白那些困扰我们很多年的复杂问题时，你会体验到欣喜若狂的感觉。

3. Science is a very exciting experience as well as a worthwhile life goal, because only those undertakings that challenge us to develop our minds and energies to attempt the

unattainable are worthy of us.

参考译文：科学是令人激动的经历，也是值得奋斗一生的目标，因为只有那些具有挑战性的事，才能提高我们的大脑和能量，去实现不可能，才使我们变得有价值。

4. If I had been given the chance to live another life as a scientist in the 21 centuries, I would study the brain and investigate the mechanism of consciousness, reasoning, logic, and memory, and I would try to understand how this marvelous machine, that evolution has developed, is capable of analyzing itself and of understanding the world and reality.

参考译文：如果在 21 世纪，我可以作为一个科学家获得重生，我将研究大脑，研究它如何产生意识，进行推理、逻辑和记忆。我要努力去研究这个玄妙的机器是如何进化，自我分析和理解世界和现实。

范文 2

词汇 Vocabulary

主旨演讲 keynote speech

原创性技术 technological originality

头部经济 top economy（特指电商时代排名靠前的）

芯片 chip

集成电路 integrated circuit

物联网 Internet of Things

永无止境 endless

人口红利 demographic dividend

高盛 Goldman Sachs

在 11 月 23 日举行的"网易未来大会"上，闫炎在主旨演讲中表示，原创性技术才是我们的未来。在他看来，大量未来投资的基金集中在新经济，尤其是头部经济、芯片、集成电路、AI、大数据、物联网、基因技术成为新宠。在他看来，从技术层面上讲，目前推动世界进步主要有两大技术：一个是 5G。5G 的出现真正带动物联网的出现，物联网的出现能使生产型的企业得到大幅度的改造和提高。此外，人类对于生命质量的提高的期盼永无止境，因此在医疗健康、基因技术等领域大有可为。而人口红利的下降，机制红利的凸显,使国企改革有了很大的机会;人类懒惰的天性和劳动力成本的上升,使得 AI、大数据和机器人成为一个重要的投资领域。

另外一个推动世界进步的技术是新型制造,闫炎非常看好5G、物联网改造制造业。他表示,从历史来看,机会都是以群的形式出现的,当 5G、基因技术出现以后,未来 5 年将会有更多机会出现。

"高盛原有的 300 多个交易员,现在只剩 2 个,绝大部分被计算机取代了。"闫炎认为,虽然 AI 人工智能出现后,30% ~ 40% 的职业可能会消失,但年轻一代聪明、踏实、有技术的原创,是中国未来经济增长最重要的推动力,所以原创性的技术才是我们的未来。"因此,中国 VC/PE 的投资前景一片灿烂,只是路途漫漫,关键是大家要活到明天。"闫炎说。

注释:

1. 而人口红利的下降,机制红利的凸显,使国企改革有了很大的机会;人类懒惰的天性和劳动力成本的上升,使得 AI、大数据和机器人成为一个重要的投资领域。

参考译文: The decline of demographic dividend and ascendance of mechanism dividend offers great opportunity for the reform of state-owned enterprises, and the idle nature of human being and the rise of labor cost endow AI and big data the significance as a field of investment.

2. 从历史来看,机会都是以群的形式出现的,当 5G、基因技术出现以后,未来 5 年将会有更多机会出现。

参考译文: History has taught us that opportunity wouldn't show up alone. When 5G and gene technology emerged, there will be accompanying opportunities in the coming five years.

3. 闫炎认为,虽然 AI 人工智能出现后,30% ~ 40% 的职业可能会消失,但年轻一代聪明、踏实、有技术的原创,是中国未来经济增长最重要的推动力,所以原创性的技术才是我们的未来。

参考译文: Yan believes that the intelligence, steadfastness and originality that mark the younger generation will be the engine for economic growth in the future, although 30 – 40 percent of jobs will disappear after the emergence of AI. So, our future lies in technological originality.

范文 3

词汇 Vocabulary

同类 species of the same kind

嗅觉 olfactory

得逞 have one's way

奸笑 sinister smile

小看 belittle

似是而非 specious

呆板僵硬 stiff and inflexible

僵尸 corpse

面无表情 have a poker face

表情 facial expression

察言观色 weigh up one's words and expressions

偏爱 partial to

面相 facial feature

奸笑 sinister smile

呆板僵硬 rigid

僵尸 zombie

脸,是一个人最显著的身体特征,我们辨认同类多依靠脸。侦探小说中经常描写凶手丢掉被害人的脑袋,受害者的身份便无从追查。辨别同类,狗靠的是鼻子,因此狗是嗅觉动物,而人是视觉动物。60% 的大脑都用于视觉信息分析,对同类面孔的识别是视觉信息分析的重要内容。尤其当人类步入文明,用衣服遮盖了身体,脸就更成为识别同类信息的主要部位。

我们的脸上布满了大大小小的表情肌肉,能做出恨、怕、愁、苦、嫉妒、震惊等 7000 种丰富的表情。不要小看这种功能,每多一种表情就会大大增强表达功能,例如"笑"。我们已经习惯了在见面时候的微笑,得逞时的奸笑,却没有意识到"笑"几乎是人类特有的专利,只有一些与人亲近的猫狗才能做出似是而非的笑容。1872 年,达尔文出版了"人类与动物的表情",这是除"物种起源"和"人类起源"外,他最重要的一部著作,书中记述了人类表情从动物表情进化来的过程。如今随着机器人的发展,很多科学家也尝试用机器人来模拟活人的表情,虽然头上布满马达,但其表情依然呆板僵硬,宛若僵尸,即使笑也让人心生恐怖。

我们不仅擅长用脸来表达,同样善于从别人脸上获取信息。所谓"察言观色"就是指从对方的表情上阅读信息,即使那人竭力掩饰,内心的变化依然在脸上有所显示。为了验证这点,加州大学心理学家保罗·艾克曼设计了著名的假笑实验。实验通过两张真假笑容的照片来验证人们分辨真假表情的能力。这种能力据说从人出生时就有,心理学家布鲁克斯就此做了一项著名实验。试验中他给婴儿出示了画着笑脸、动物和抽象的几何图形的图片。实验发现即使是两个月大的婴儿也对面孔图案特别偏爱。另一位心理学家—英国的奥利弗更发现,6个月大的婴儿对不同种族人类的识别能力甚至胜于成人,这也证明出于进化的考虑,人类的基因中已经积累了大量的对于面孔的经验。脸上承载信息之多,以至古今中外的算命先生都要看脸,从而也就有"相面"之说。估计人类这种辨识训练从还是猴子时就已开始。科学实验发现,人类对一张恐惧的脸的反应速度是对一般脸的三倍。这应该源于我们时常要从同伴身上发现临近的危险,对脸反应的速度决定了我们的存亡。

注释:

1. 60%的大脑都用于视觉信息分析,对同类面孔的识别是视觉信息分析的重要内容。

参考译文:60% of our brain is contributed to analysis of visual information, and identifying the faces of species of the same kind is an important part of that.

2. 不要小看这种功能,每多一种表情就会大大增强表达功能,例如"笑"。

参考译文:Never belittle such function, for one additional facial expression will enhance our expressiveness largely, just as illustrated by our smile.

3. 如今随着机器人的发展,很多科学家也尝试用机器人来模拟活人的表情,虽然头上布满马达,但其表情依然呆板僵硬,宛若僵尸,即使笑也让人心生恐怖。

参考译文：The progress in robotics enables simulation of human facial expression experimented by scientists. With motors placed everywhere on the head, but their facial expression remains stiff and inflexible like corpse, frightening even when smiling.

4. 所谓"察言观色"就是指从对方的表情上阅读信息，即使那人竭力掩饰，内心的变化依然在脸上有所显示。

参考译文：To read his face and to weigh his words is so expressed as you can acquire information from a person's facial expression, even if he's trying to cover up, his mind will still be revealed by his face.

范文 4

词汇 Vocabulary

头疼的问题 headache

全球变暖 global warming

横空出世 jump start；roar across the horizon

末世感 apocalyptic vertigo；feel of doomsday

刻不容缓 pressing；waiting for no delay

话语权 right of speech

脑死亡 brain death

气候变化问题可谓是全球最让人头疼的问题了，自全球变暖发生以来，各国媒体便开始一次又一次地将全球变暖和自然灾害联系在一起，而不久以前的气候少女格雷诺的横空出世，更是加剧了这一末世感，让人人自危。今日欧洲议会召开就气候紧急状态一事进行讨论的大会，此次会议的主题是，欧洲如何应对接下来的气候环境。

根据会议调查，目前全球气候变暖问题已经到了刻不容缓的地步，包括两极冰面、全球山火问题及洪涝自然灾害都是全球变暖所产生的恶果，人类必须肩负起保护环境的责任，而非放任这一恶果。而如何肩负起这一责任，欧洲必须带领全人类走出一片新天地，因此，欧洲议会启动"气候紧急状态"，通过该状态，呼吁欧洲人以及全人类重视气候环境变化带来的影响。而这一决议也以压倒性投票通过,欧洲议会成员国宣布进入气候紧急状态。据了解,该决议并不具有直接法律约束力,但仍是有力的信号,它代表了欧洲议会终于正视了气候问题,并对外释放一个强烈信号,那就是环保问题刻不容缓。

当然,这也是欧洲重夺话语权的重要一步。近几年,由于美国影响力下降,才让欧洲国家重新活跃起来,其中法国、德国更是多次试图夺回领导权。在前不久,法国总统马克龙曾直言北约已经"脑死亡",而对于这次会议的举办,马克龙更是起到推动作用。可以说,此次会议既是一次决定了欧洲在有关气候的问题上的影响力的会议,也是以马克龙为代表的新生代欧洲领导人重夺世界话语权的第一步。

注释:

1. 气候变化问题可谓是全球最让人头疼的问题了,自全球变暖发生以来,各国媒体便开始一次又一次地将全球变暖和自然灾害联系在一起,而不久以前的气候少女格雷诺的横空出世,更是加剧了这一末世感,让人人自危。

参考译文: Climate change is the worst headache of the world. Media in different nations try to associate global warming with the natural disasters once and again, and the emergence of Greenow, the Ms. Climate exacerbated the feeling of doomsday that put everyone in anxiety.

2. 据了解,该决议并不具有直接法律约束力,但仍是有力的信号,它代表了欧洲议会终于正视了气候问题,并对外释放一个强烈信号,那就是环保问题刻不容缓。

参考译文: It is given to understand that the resolution has no legal binding, yet still a strong signal that European Convention takes seriously the climate challenge, and its attitude is shown that the environmental issue waits for no one.

3. 可以说,此次会议既是一次决定了欧洲在有关气候问题上的影响力的会议,也是以马克龙为代表的新生代欧洲领导人重夺世界话语权的第一步。

参考译文: It is righteous to say that the conference is both

an event that determines the influence of Europe in climate-related issue, and the first move taken by the new generation of European leaders trying to voice their opinions.

第十章 艺 术

范文 1

词汇 Vocabulary

Cluster 聚集体

Lille 里尔

Nerve center 神经中枢

Corrugated 波纹的

Polyester 聚酯纤维

Congestion 阻塞

Straddling 骑跨

Complex 建筑群

Prestigious 知名的

Austere 简约的；简朴的

Monastic 寺庙的

In the guise of 隐藏的

Hanshin 阪神

Kobe 神户

Osaka 大阪

Intact 未受损害

Triennial 三年一次的

The most-talked-about work of architecture and engineering in the year was what some called "the crossroads of Europe," the immense new cluster of buildings at the entrance to the Channel Tunnel (Eurotunnel) in Lille, France.

The complex, known as Eurallille, was one hour from Paris and two hours from London by train. It was to be linked by high-speed rail to Amsterdam; Brussels; Cologne, Germany; and other parts of Europe in the future and would likely serve as the nerve center for a multinational community of 100 million people. Parts of Eurallile opened in 1999 and 2000, but much was still under construction, Dutch architect Rem Koolhaas created the master plan for Eurallile. He also designed in vast Grand Palais, or Congrexpo, which included a conference center, an exhibit hall, and an arena for rock concerts. Koolhaas gave each of them a different architectural appearance, using industrial materials such as corrugated polyester and aluminum, in order to create a sense of random collision and congestion— qualities that he admired and that were described in his book *Delirious New York*.

Other buildings, straddling the station for the TGV (Train a Grande Vitese), included a slope-sided Credit-Lyonnais bank tower by French architect Christian de Portzamparc and Eurallile Center, a vast complex by Frenchman Jean Nouvel that included stores, restaurants, theaters, a business school, a sports center, and residential apartments. Hotels, parks, and a world trade center wee also planed for Eurallile.

Tadao Ando of Japan was the 1999 winner of the most prestigious international award in the field, the \$100,000 Pritzker Architecture Prize. Already widely honored, Ando was known for an austere, almost monastic type of architecture, usually built of beautifully finished raw concrete, often in simple geometric shapes, and without any ornament or historic detail. "I do not believe architecture should speak too much." Ando had said. "It should remain silent and let nature in the guise of sunlight and wind speak. A believer in solid construction, Ando proudly announced that after the destructive January 17 Great Hanshin Earthquake in the Kobe area, Japan, all of his 30 buildings in the quake zone remained intact. One of the architect's major works was the Suntory Museum in Osaka, which opened during 1995 and contained spaces for housing contemporary art and for staging performing art.

In an unusual move the Royal Institute of British Architects gave its Gold Medal to a teacher and critic rather than an architect: Colin Rowe, a British-born professor of architecture at Cornell University, NY. The triennial Aga Khan Awards for Architecture were presented for 12 works of Islamic architecture, ranging from the reconstruction of historic neighborhoods to the design of an environmentally sensitive office tower. The Mier van der Hohe Pavilion Award for European Architecture was given to Nicholas Grimshaw's waterloo International Terminal, the British link to the Channel Tunnel. The American Institute of Architects did not award its Gold Medal in 1995. The winner of the AIA's Twenty-Five Year Award for 1996 was announced. Given annually to a building that has proved its worth over time, the award went to the 1962 Air Force Academy Cadet Chapel in Colorado Springs, Colo. By skidmore.

注释：

1. The most talked-about work of architecture and engineering in the year was what some called "the crossroads of Europe", the immense new cluster of buildings at the entrance to the Channel Tunnel(Rurotunnel)in Lille, France.

参考译文：本年度话题度最高的建筑和工程是被称为"欧洲十字路口"的巨型建筑群,位于法国里尔的海峡隧道(欧洲隧道)入口。

第十章 艺 术

2. Koolhaas gave each of them a different architectural appearance, using industrial materials such as corrugated polyester and aluminum, in order to create a sense of random collision and congestion—qualities that he admired and that were described in his book Delirious New York.

参考译文：库哈斯赋予每个建筑不同的外观,他应用了各种工业材料,如波纹型的聚酯材料和铝,目的是创造出随意冲突和聚集感。这种风格是他所崇尚的,并在他那本名为"疯狂纽约"的书中进行了描述。

3. Already widely honored, Ando was known for an autere, almost monastic type of architecture, usually built of beautifully finished raw concrete, often simple geometric shapes, and without any ornament or historic detail.

参考译文：安藤已经是广受赞誉的建筑师,他以简约,近似寺庙式的建筑风格而闻名。他经常把进行了美观处理的混凝土作为材料,将建筑设计成简单的几何形状,不用任何装饰或不呈现历史细节。

范文 2

词汇 Vocabulary

chef 专业厨师

cuisine 烹饪

eatery 餐馆

apprehensive 忧虑

gird 一束；捆上

shun 避开

stock 原汤

taste-bug 美食家

upscale 迎合高层消费者的

simmer 慢炖

lemongrass 柠檬草

fusion cuisine 混合烹饪

rich 多油味道浓的

choucroute 泡菜

cassoulet 豆炖肉

bouillabaisse 法式杂鱼汤

hollandaise 荷兰酸辣酱

beurre blanc 黄油白沙司

braise 用文火炖

pot-au-feu 蔬菜牛肉浓汤

junk food 高脂肪小吃

latte 拿铁咖啡

tinker 瞎摆弄

flair 天赋

Parisians 巴黎人

ambience 环境

A. 当初你在巴黎开店心里是不是有点发怵?

B. I was a little afraid. But it was always in the back of my mind to come back one day and do something here. I wanted to bring my experience of 15 years in New York to Paris, to do something with American flair and energy. Five years ago, I wouldn't have even dared. But now Parisians are more and more like Americans—going out five, six times a week. They want traditional brasseries, and they are open to new ideas, to a good time and a good ambience.

A. 您在美国学到的什么最重要?

B.Communication. French chefs are very—not close-minded—but focused. My chef here is an American. I needed someone that is open-minded and flexible. The old-time chefs in France are very "do-it-my-way."

A. 就像当初您效力的那些厨师一样?

B. Yeah. I was very lucky to work with these men. But each time I went to another one, I had to erase everything I had learned from the one I had just left, like the way they peeled apples and potatoes. It was about one person's way of doing things. I was like that for a little while, too, but I changed because you learn so much from your colleagues. My kitchen is more like a democracy now. If someone has am idea, I want to hear it, see it. I want to taste it.

A. 就正餐而言,美国和法国有什么不同?

B. The kitchen is still very new in America, historically speaking—so people there are willing to try new things. The traditions aren't set like they are in France.

A. 您把亚洲学到的什么带到了纽约?

B. Asia was a culture shock. It changed my mind completely. I was used to cooking with stocks that would simmer for hours and hours. In Asia everything is in a pot of water. Throw in some spices, lemongrass and 10 minutes later you have the best soup in the world. I put my French training away for a while and learned.

A. 您认为混合式烹调——就像您的法—泰混合式烹调——的趋势会最终取代传统烹调吗?

B. No, I don't think so. Take French food. Some say French food is too rich. But that's Auguste Escoffier's style of cooking, and in the end, Escoffier was one guy who did really fine hotel food. The true French cooking for me is regional food: choucroute from Alsace, cassoulet from the southwest, bouillabaisse from Provence, and there isn't cream and butter in any of it. I never had a hollandaise or beurre blanc when I was growing up. It was braised meats, pot-au-feu. I'm not anti-Escoffier, but how can one person qualify French cooking? He may have been right at time, but not any more.

A. 您最喜欢什么饮食?

B. Thai street food, from the carts in Bangkok. It has so much flavor. That's my junk food.

A. 哪些是您最爱光顾的餐馆?

B. In New York I love Daniel Boulud's Restaurant, Daniel and Tom Colicchio's Craft, where you choose exactly what you want—your meat, your vegetables, everything—piece by piece. I go to Starbucks every morning and get my grande latte.

I love Starbucks. In Paris I love Arpege. The chef Alain Passard is really an artist. In London there's an Indian restaurant called Tamarind that does beautiful food. In Bangkok it's street food—always. And the best Chinese food in Hong Kong is Man Wa. It's so important for a chef to travel. You get so inspired. I go to Asia two or three times a year and come back with 20 or 30 recipes.

A. 在您的餐馆里您还亲自动手吗?

B. That's my therapy. I like to do business. I like to be involved in the design. But I need my six hours of therapy every day, in every town. I test-cook, come up with new dishes and tinker. I wouldn't feel comfortable if I didn't spend a couple of hours in the kitchen each day. I may not run the marathon anymore. But I do the 200 meters. I need the rush.

注释:

1. I was used to cooking with stocks that would simmer for hours and hours.

参考译文: 我原来用老汤烹饪,慢炖几个小时。

2. Thai street food, from the carts in Bangkok. It has so much flavor. That's my junk food.

参考译文: 泰国街头食品,像曼谷的路边小吃,口味颇多,是我的最爱。

范文 3

词汇 Vocabulary

全景画 panorama

后起的 up-and-coming; budding

风靡 take...by storm; sweep...

认知性 cognition

意识形态 ideology; mentality

恢宏的气势 tremendous momentum

画布 canvas

得天独厚的 abound in gift of nature

临场感 on-the-spot experience

环形叙事 circular narration

线性叙事 linear narration

拟真 simulation

地面塑形 foreground molding

崇高 loftiness

作为一种艺术形式,全景画自 18 世纪后期诞生以来,迅速风靡西欧,又很快在俄国、美国、日本等国广为流传,直到电影、电视等新兴大众传媒崛起,使其经历了近半个世纪的消歇,最终于 20 世纪 50 年代又重新回到历史现场。中国全景画的发展始于 20 世纪 80 年代,经过几十年,取得了长足进步,不论在组织上、技术上、艺术性上,还是在全景画的保存、维护及修复上都达到了世界先进水平。

从艺术分类上讲,全景画属于大众文化艺术形式。作为现代工业化、都市化进程影响下的大众艺术,全景画从诞生之初,就显现着鲜明的大众文化传播媒介特质和消费文化特征。它的"公共性"既体现在对时事、历史事件、风光等的传播,满足大众的认知性、娱乐性需求上,又与意识形态有着密切的关联。全景画其求真的审美追求、恢宏的气势、庞大的规模,特别适合于对重大历史题材和意识形态、政治诉求的呈现和传播。

从媒介上看,全景画不局限在画布上,打破了二维平面的局限,是一种建立在三维空间的艺术,在空间感上有得天独厚的优势。这也决定了"拟真",即"最大限度地忠实于所呈现对象",成为其独特的审美品格。为了还原所呈现对象(历史、时事、风景)的"真实",全景画不遗余力地捕捉每一个细节,关注观众的临场感受也是全景画有别于其他艺术形式的特征之一。为了使观众产生"身临其境"的"临场感",全景画采取了一系列技术手段,用以加强自身的艺术效果,如光与声音的运用、地面塑形的空间延展等。

全景画在美学形态上,主要呈现为一种"崇高"之美。崇高美具有严峻、冲突、巨大的体积和巨大的力量之特点,全景画尺寸巨大,场面恢宏,壮丽雄伟的场景动人心魄,营造出崇高宏伟的艺术境界。这也与全景画所经常呈现的主题有关。景观主题、历史及战争主题、宗教主题等是全景画的"擅长"领域。关于这些主题的美学叙事,主要表现为情节的选择与构置、叙事形态等方面。

在情节的选择与构置上,全景画多以典型场景、典型事件和精彩瞬间来烘托主题;同时,全景画的叙事形态也以环形叙事方式和线性叙事结构有机结合展现其独特的艺术魅力。

全景画的创作一直与科技的发展密不可分,始终受到科技的影响,而且这种影响又是多元的。从技术层面讲,对科学透视法则的把握和运用是全景画的主要创作原则。全景画在传统艺术科学透视法则的基础之上,发展出独特的旋转环视画面的特殊艺术形式,并且赋予了绘画透视学一种新的理论活力。此外,特殊的展出场馆,音乐、解说、各种模拟声响以及灯光照明等艺术手段的运用,都增加了全景画的拟真效果。

全景画的审美实现实际上是一种创作与观赏之间的互动。一方面,全景画的自我创造、表现形式和技巧甚至呈现内容等并非预先设定,而是在与观赏者的互动中,在大众的观赏与品评,逐渐习得并不断调整、完善的。"学会表现"与创造"自我"是全景画创作主体建构及审美实现相辅相成的两个面向。另一方面,观众的审美实现是通过"临场感"的获得来完成的。为观众提供"艺术的享受""心灵的震撼""情感的升华""历史的感悟",是全景画实现其审美认知和审美教育的关键所在。

综上,可以认为,全景画是一种集空间结构与时间结构、集视觉与听觉、集史学与文学的综合性艺术样式。它借助于多元的技术手段展开对所表现对象的立体在线,并融合了想象实现视觉元素、听觉元素构建其自身艺术结构。

注释:

作为一种艺术形式,全景画自 18 世纪后期诞生以来,迅速风靡西欧,又很快在俄国、美国、日本等国广为流传,直到电影、电视等新兴大众传媒崛起,方经历了近半个世纪的消歇,最终于 20 世纪 50 年代又重新回到历史现场。

参考译文: As an art form, panorama swept Western Europe after its birth in the 18th century, and stormed Russia, USA and Japan until the emergence of motion pictures and Television. It came back to the historic scene in the 1950s after half a century of pause.

范文 4

词汇 Vocabulary

都督府 military commander of province

赔款 reparation

游牧民族 nomads

中原 mid-China

首领 chieftain

出土 excavate; unearth

矿冶 mining and metallurgy

汉化 sinicized

陈国公主墓出土于内蒙古,其墓主人是辽景帝的孙女,墓中出土金银器 50 多件,是辽代墓葬中出土文物最丰富的贵族墓。出土的这些金银器中大部分都具有游牧民族风格,也融合了中原文化特征。

在辽国早期遗物中,中原风格往往与契丹风格并存,这是因为契丹和唐朝关系紧密。公元 648 年,唐设松漠都督府,由契丹联盟首领任都督。此时辽已部分接受了汉文化。辽中期,契丹贵族开始大规模效仿中原扶持农业生产的做法,同时矿冶、陶瓷、织造等行业走向新生,而融合了中原特点的契丹金银器,也开始丰富、多样化。

北宋初年,宋朝屡次对辽用兵,均以失败告终。公元 1001 年,宋朝在此兵败,开始每年向辽供绢、银等,这些赔款使辽的财政状况得到改善,生产技术和科学技术也得到有力支持。加之契丹人不断深入中原,进行贸易往来,包括金银器的流通,汉文化和契丹文化的融合达到高峰。

另外,战争中俘虏的很多中原人中,有很多手工业者,他们流入辽地后所带来的各种生产技术和审美观点,也渗透到金银器的制造中,契丹文化或多或少地被汉化了。

注释:

1. 在辽国早期遗物中,中原风格往往与契丹风格并存,这是因为契丹和唐朝关系紧密。

参考译文: Early relics of Liao Dynasty reveals the coexistence of Middle China and Qidan genre because of the intimate relationship between Qidan and the Tang Dynasty.

2. 辽中期，契丹贵族开始大规模效仿中原扶持农业生产的做法，同时矿冶、陶瓷、织造等行业走向新生，而融合了中原特点的契丹金银器，也开始丰富、多样化。

参考译文: During the Mid-Liao Dynasty period, the Qidan aristocrats started massive simulation of the pro-agriculture policy carried out by Middle China, meanwhile mining, metallurgy, ceramics-making and textile revived, while goldware and silverware mingled with Middle China style budded with diversity.

3. 公元 1001 年，宋朝在此兵败，开始每年向辽供绢、银等，这些赔款使辽的财政状况得到改善，生产技术和科学技术也得到有力支持。

参考译文: The Song Dynasty was defeated in 1001 AD, which was followed by annual tribute to Liao Dynasty, the winner, and that contributed to improved fiscal condition of Liao, hence the agriculture and technology were correspondingly supported as well.

范文 5

词汇 Vocabulary

take ... by storm 风靡……

witchcraft 巫术

blockbuster 大片

wizardry 魔术

antiquated 过气的

manuscript 手写本

audition 试听

aerial combat 空中格斗

dungeons 土牢

staging 演出

lavish 宏大奢华

shrine 圣地

voice break 变声

Last Thursday, the day before I got on the plane to fly to China, I went to see a movie. It wasn't just any movie, but the recent Harry Potter blockbuster "The Philosopher's Stone" that has taken Britain, America and now Japan by storm.

The film is a fabulous tale of witchcraft and wizardry set in modern-day Britain. Based on a book by J.K. Rowling, it tells the story of a very special baby, scarred at birth by an evil wizard who kills his parents. The only legacy of the tragedy is a red mark on the baby's forehead—and magic power, inherited from his mother and father, to combat and overcome evil.

Antiquated as this sounds, in fact the Harry Potter myth was founded just 5 years ago by Joanne Rowling, a poor single mother living in Edinburgh, in the north of the United Kingdom. To date, 110 million copies of her books have been sold worldwide. But before her publisher would accept the first manuscript, Joanne Rowling had to agree to change her name on the book cover to J.K. Rowling because it was feared that children, particularly young boys, would not read an adventure story written by a woman. Only later, when the books became an overnight success, did it become generally known that the talented and creative author was in fact a young and attractive woman.

The original idea came to Joanne whilst traveling on a long train journey across England. Harry Potter appeared to her "fully formed" and she is quoted as saying that Daniel Radcliffe, the actor who plays Harry in the movie, "is a truly miraculous find" and that "he embodies the soul of Harry Potter".

At the start of production, forty thousand child actors were auditioned and tested for the screen role, yet Daniel Radcliffe was discovered when the producers took a break and went out to a theater in London's west end. There in the next row sat young Daniel who was visiting the theater with his father for an evening's entertainment. Daniel was screen tested and with J.K.

Rowling's full approval was immediately offered the part.

The film is wonderfully spectacular, there's no doubt about that. The visual effects, which range from aerial combat with broomsticks to a scary three-headed monster raging and roaring deep within the school's dungeons, never ceased to thrill and inspire. The staging is lavish, and backgrounds for the film have been based on some of the finest old buildings from around the United Kingdom.

It's not surprising, with the huge popularity of the first movie, that many of these locations have now become shrines to Hogwarts. Recently, avid children accompanied by their eager parents have been visiting to touch into some of the local magic of Harry Potter.

A second movie is now in production, which the producers are desperately trying to complete before child actor Daniel Radcliffe's voice breaks.

注释:

1. It wasn't just any movie, but the recent Harry Potter blockbuster "The Philosopher's Stone" that has taken Britain, America and now Japan by storm.

参考译文: 它可不是一般的电影, 而是最近风靡英国、美国和日本的大片"哈利·波特和魔法石"。

2. Harry Potter appeared to her "fully formed" and she is quoted as saying that Daniel Radcliffe, the actor who plays Harry in the movie, "is a truly miraculous find" and that "he embodies the soul of Harry Potter".

参考译文: 哈利·波特形象在她的脑海中丰满起来, 引用作者的话: 扮演哈利·波特的演员丹尼尔·拉德克里夫"简直是个奇迹的发现", "他赋予哈利·波特这个人物以生命。"

3. The visual effects, which range from aerial combat with broomsticks to a scary three-headed monster raging and roaring deep within the school's dungeons, never ceased to thrill and inspire.

参考译文：从骑着扫把进行空中格斗到学校地牢深处咆哮暴怒的三头怪兽，影片的视效自始至终令人震颤和遐想。